Modern Middle East Nations

AND THEIR STRATEGIC PLACE IN THE WORLD

QATAR

Modern Middle East Nations
AND THEIR STRATEGIC PLACE IN THE WORLD

QATAR

LISA McCOY

MASON CREST PUBLISHERS
PHILADELPHIA

Produced by OTTN Publishing, Stockton, New Jersey

Mason Crest Publishers
370 Reed Road
Broomall, PA 19008
www.masoncrest.com

First printing

1 3 5 7 9 8 6 4 2

Library of Congress Cataloging-in-Publication Data

McCoy, Lisa.
  Qatar / Lisa McCoy.
      p. cm. — (Modern Middle East nations and their strategic place
in the world)
Summary: Discusses the geography, history, economy, government,
religion, people, foreign relations, and communities of Qatar.
Includes bibliographical references and index.
  ISBN 1-59084-523-4
1. Qatar—Juvenile literature. [1. Qatar.] I. Title. II. Series.
DS247.Q3M397 2003
953.63—dc21
                                        2003000902

TABLE OF CONTENTS

Modern Middle East Nations
AND THEIR STRATEGIC PLACE IN THE WORLD

Dr. Harvey Sicherman, president and director of the Foreign Policy Research Institute, is the author of such books as *America the Vulnerable: Our Military Problems and How to Fix Them* (2002) and *Palestinian Autonomy, Self-Government and Peace* (1993).

Introduction

by Dr. Harvey Sicherman

Situated as it is between Africa, Europe, and the Far East, the Middle East has played a unique role in world history. Often described as the birthplace of religions (notably Judaism, Christianity, and Islam) and the cradle of civilizations (Egypt, Mesopotamia, Persia), this region and its peoples have given humanity some of its most precious possessions. At the same time, the Middle East has had more than its share of conflicts. The area is strewn with the ruins of fortifications and the cemeteries of combatants, not to speak of modern arsenals for war.

Today, more than ever, Americans are aware that events in the Middle East can affect our security and prosperity. The United States has a considerable military, political, and economic presence throughout much of the region. Developments there regularly find their way onto the front pages of our newspapers and the screens of our television sets.

Still, it is fair to say that most Middle Eastern countries remain a mystery, their cultures and religions barely known, their peoples and politics confusing and strange. The purpose of this book series is to change that, to educate the reader in the basic facts about the 23 states and many peoples that make up the region. (For our purpose, the Middle East also includes the North African states linked by ethnicity, language, and religion to the Arabs, as well as Somalia and Mauritania, which are African but share the Muslim religion and are members of the Arab League.) A notable feature of the series is the integration of geography, demography, and history; economics and politics; culture and religion. The careful student will learn much that he or she needs to know about ever so important lands.

A few general observations are in order as an introduction to the subject matter.

The first has to do with history and politics. The modern Middle East is full of ancient sites and peoples who trace their lineage and literature to antiquity. Many commentators also attribute the Middle East's political conflicts to grievances and rivalries from the distant past. While history is often invoked, the truth is that the modern Middle East political system dates only from the 1920s and was largely created by the British and the French, the victors of World War I. Such states as Algeria, Iraq, Israel, Jordan, Kuwait, Saudi Arabia, Syria, Turkey, and the United Arab Emirates did not exist before 1914—they became independent between 1920 and 1971. Others, such as Egypt and Iran, were dominated by outside powers until well after World War II. Before 1914, most of the region's states were either controlled by the Turkish-run Ottoman Empire or owed allegiance to the Ottoman sultan. (The sultan was also the caliph or highest religious authority in Islam, in the line of the prophet Muhammad's successors, according to the beliefs of the majority of Muslims known as the Sunni.) It was this imperial Muslim system that was ended by the largely British military victory over the Ottomans in World War I. Few of the leaders who emerged in the wake of this event were happy with the territories they were assigned or the borders, which were often drawn by Europeans. Yet, the system has endured despite many efforts to change it.

The second observation has to do with economics, demography, and natural resources. The Middle Eastern peoples live in a region of often dramatic geographical contrasts: vast parched deserts and high mountains, some with year-round snow; stone-hard volcanic rifts and lush semi-tropical valleys; extremely dry and extremely wet conditions, sometimes separated by only a few miles; large permanent rivers and wadis, riverbeds dry as a bone until winter rains send torrents of flood from the mountains to the sea. In ancient times, a very skilled agriculture made the Middle East the breadbasket of the Roman Empire, and its trade carried luxury fabrics, foods, and spices both East and West.

Most recently, however, the Middle East has become more known for a single commodity—oil, which is unevenly distributed and largely concentrated in the Persian Gulf and Arabian Peninsula (although large pockets are also to be found in Algeria, Libya, and other sites). There are also new, potentially lucrative offshore gas fields in the Eastern Mediterranean.

This uneven distribution of wealth has been compounded by demographics. Birth rates are very high, but the countries with the most oil are often lightly populated. Over the last decade, Middle East populations under the age of 20 have grown enormously. How will these young people be educated? Where will they work? The failure of most governments in the region to give their people skills and jobs (with notable exceptions such as Israel) has also contributed to large out-migrations. Many have gone to Europe; many others work in other Middle Eastern countries, supporting their families from afar.

Another unsettling situation is the heavy pressure both people and industry have put on vital resources. Chronic water shortages plague the region. Air quality, public sanitation, and health services in the big cities are also seriously overburdened. There are solutions to these problems, but they require a cooperative approach that is sorely lacking.

A third important observation is the role of religion in the Middle East. Americans, who take separation of church and state for granted, should know that most countries in the region either proclaim their countries to be Muslim or allow a very large role for that religion in public life. Among those with predominantly Muslim populations, Turkey alone describes itself as secular and prohibits avowedly religious parties in the political system. Lebanon was a Christian-dominated state, and Israel continues to be a Jewish state. While both strongly emphasize secular politics, religion plays an enormous role in culture, daily life, and legislation. It is also important to recall that Islamic law (*Sharia*) permits people to practice Judaism and Christianity in Muslim states but only as *Dhimmi*, protected but very second-class citizens.

Fourth, the American student of the modern Middle East will be impressed by the varieties of one-man, centralized rule, very unlike the workings of Western democracies. There are monarchies, some with traditional methods of consultation for tribal elders and even ordinary citizens, in Saudi Arabia and many Gulf States; kings with limited but still important parliaments (such as in Jordan and

Morocco); and military and civilian dictatorships, some (such as Syria) even operating on the hereditary principle (Hafez al Assad's son Bashar succeeded him). Turkey is a practicing democracy, although a special role is given to the military that limits what any government can do. Israel operates the freest democracy, albeit constricted by emergency regulations (such as military censorship) due to the Arab-Israeli conflict.

In conclusion, the MODERN MIDDLE EAST NATIONS series will engage imagination and interest simply because it covers an area of such great importance to the United States. Americans may be relative latecomers to the affairs of this region, but our involvement there will endure. We at the Foreign Policy Research Institute hope that these books will kindle a lifelong interest in the fascinating and significant Middle East.

A young Arab boy in traditional dress holds the reins of a muzzled camel at the Abrega camel race course, Qatar. In recent years this country on the edge of the Arabian Peninsula has become more important than its small size would indicate.

Place in the World

Qatar (pronounced "cutter" or "gutter") is one of the smallest territories in the Middle East. As a result, throughout history it has often been overlooked. Some maps of the region drawn before the 19th century do not even show the Qatar **Peninsula**, which juts off the Arabian Peninsula into the Arabian Gulf. Qatar is located on the peninsula, and also controls a number of small islands in the Arabian Gulf. The country's entire land area is smaller than the state of Connecticut.

Until the 20th century, most observers perceived the Qatar Peninsula as worthless desert. Qatar is bordered by Saudi Arabia and the United Arab Emirates to the south and by the Arabian Gulf to the north, east, and west. The land is primarily flat and barren, with sand and rock covering much of the territory. Because Qatar lacks any permanent bodies of water such as streams, lakes, or rivers, most of its water supply comes either from underground **aquifers** or man-made **desalinization** plants. There is little plant or animal life.

Qatar might have remained a poor desert nation were it not for the discovery of oil in the Gulf region. Today, the country is a major producer of both petroleum and natural gas, two natural resources that are needed to fuel the economies of industrially developed countries. Revenues from oil and gas have helped transform Qatar from a desert backwater into a modern country, and given citizens of the country a standard of living that is among the highest in the world.

The country's production of oil and natural gas is one reason tiny Qatar is more important than many nations that are much larger and are home to many more people. Another reason for Qatar's importance is its location in the Middle East, a region that has been in turmoil for decades. Long before Qatar became an independent country in the early 1970s, violence and unrest were common in the Middle East. The Arab states of this region have often clashed with each other, and have fought wars with neighbors like Iran and Israel.

Qatar has found that it cannot always stay out of territorial disputes with its neighbors. For many years the country was involved in a dispute with Bahrain over the Hawar Islands. Qatar has also had boundary disputes with Saudi Arabia and the United Arab Emirates. In addition, political conflicts among the other Gulf States—such as the Iran-Iraq War (1980–88) and the Iraqi invasion of Kuwait and the Gulf War that followed (1990–91)—have affected Qatar and its policies over the years. Despite these occasional problems, the government of Qatar has tried to maintain a policy of openness and friendship with other countries. It was a founding member of the Gulf Cooperation Council (GCC), which brought the Gulf States together for mutual defense and economic development.

Because of Qatar's strategic location, U.S. forces have been based in the country since the early 1990s in the event that war

U.S. Secretary of Defense Donald H. Rumsfeld (left) and Qatari Minister of Foreign Affairs Hamad ibn Jasim al-Thani sign a defense agreement on December 11, 2002, in Wabah Palace in Doha, Qatar. The agreement allowed the United States to expand its presence at the al-Udeid air base and upgrade other facilities in Qatar. Mutual defense agreements like this one have made the small country an important strategic partner of the United States in the Arabian Gulf region.

breaks out in the region. In 2002, Qatar and the United States signed a defense agreement in which the U.S. was given permission to expand its presence at key Qatari bases. This was particularly significant as it came at a time when the U.S. was preparing for war with another Arabian Gulf country, Iraq. Although some Arabs condemned the defense agreement, the Qatari bases were considered crucial for U.S. operations against Iraq, particularly after the government of Saudi Arabia expressed reservations about allowing U.S. troops to use bases in that country for an attack.

Finally, the government of Qatar has been willing to follow a

Palestinians watch an Al-Jazeera television broadcast, which showed the videotaped will of one of the men who carried out the September 11, 2001, attack on the World Trade Center and Pentagon in the United States. Al-Jazeera has been criticized by leaders of many Arab countries for its controversial programming, while Western leaders have argued that the station acts as a "mouthpiece" for Osama bin Laden and other terrorist leaders. Nontheless, Al-Jazeera's programs have made it extremely popular among Arab television viewers.

more moderate path than many of its Arab neighbors. Since 1995, under the leadership of Emir Hamad ibn Khalifa al-Thani, Qatar has eliminated some government restrictions, including censorship of the press. Since 1996 the Al-Jazeera television network, which is based in Qatar, has become one of the most popular sources of programming in the Arab world because of its various shows on which controversial issues are openly debated—a rarity in the Arab world. And in March 1999 Qatar held municipal elections, becoming the second Arab state in the Gulf region to hold open elections in more than 20 years.

As Qatar steps onto the world stage and plays a more active role in political events, it will be interesting to see how this small desert nation makes the most of its resources and strategic position.

A waterfall in the desert on the Qatar Peninsula. The small peninsula is mostly desert, and water is a rare commodity.

The Land

The State of Qatar (Dawlat Qatar) is located on a peninsula that itself is located on a peninsula. The small Qatar Peninsula varies in width; it is about 56 miles (90 kilometers) across at its widest point and approximately 34 miles (55 km) across at its narrowest. The Qatar Peninsula extends off the eastern coast of the larger Arabian Peninsula, jutting some 99 miles (160 km) into the Arabian Gulf. Qatar, which takes up the peninsula as well as some smaller islands in the Gulf, covers an area of 4,416 square miles (11,437 sq km).

For the most part, the land of the Qatar Peninsula is low-lying desert. The highest point in the country is just 338 feet (103 meters) at Qurayn Abu al Bawl. Much of the country is covered with sand or loose gravel; some areas are quite rocky. Massive sand dunes surround Khor al-Udeid (in English, the Inland Sea), a large bay on the southeast coast of the Qatar Peninsula that has a narrow connection to the Gulf. Another unique feature appears along the west coast of Qatar—elevated limestone formations called the Dukhan **anticline**. Under this region lies the Dukhan oil field, the largest oil field in Qatar.

Salt-encrusted basins are common in the coastal areas of Qatar, particularly in the south and east of the country. A *sabkhah* (an Arabic term meaning "salt flat") is a depression in the desert floor that contains fine-grained deposits of silt, sand, or clay. *Sibakh* (the plural form of *sabkhah*) are formed by the evaporation of salt water. They can cause problems for people traveling through the desert. When the *sibakh* are dry, the salt basins can support the weight of a vehicle, but if they become wet, even small trucks can sink deep into the ooze.

Of the offshore territories belonging to Qatar, the island of Halul is the most important. Less than 0.6 square miles in size (about 1.5 sq km), Halul is located about 56 miles (90 km) east of Doha, the capital of Qatar. The island serves primarily as a place where crude

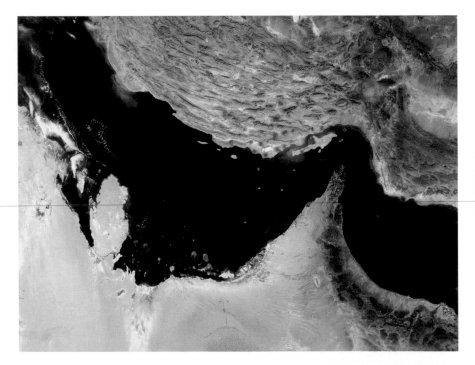

An overview of the Arabian Gulf shows the Qatar Peninsula, which is to the left of center in this photograph. The area to the right of the peninsula where the waterway narrows is the Strait of Hormuz.

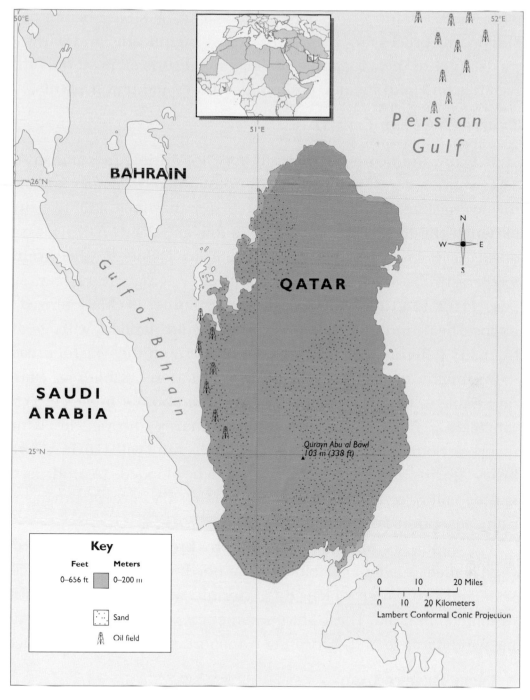

As this map indicates, much of the Qatar Peninsula is low-lying desert. The major oil fields are in the west of the country in the Dukhan region. Offshore oil fields, and the country's largest reserve of natural gas, the North Field, are located in the Gulf to the north.

oil from the country's offshore oil fields can be stored before being shipped to processing plants. The most significant landmarks on the island are the 11 giant tanks in which crude oil is stored; other facilities on Halul include pumping stations and power plants.

TEMPERATURE AND CLIMATE

In Qatar the weather is typically very hot during the summer, but somewhat moderate during the winter. Between November and May, the average temperature is about 73° Fahrenheit (23° Celsius), although the temperature can fall as low as 62°F (17°C). However, during the long summer (early June to October), the average temperature is above 95°F (35°C) and daily temperatures can surpass 110°F (43°C) in July and August. Summer is characterized by intense heat and alternating dry and humid periods, with greater humidity (often reaching 90 percent or more) in the coastal areas.

As might be expected in a desert nation, rainfall is hardly noticeable in Qatar. Precipitation averages about 4 inches (10 centimeters) per year. The rain falls primarily during the winter months. Sometimes, all of the country's rain will fall in a brief, heavy storm, and the **wadis** will become flooded. (A wadi is the bed or valley of a stream that is usually dry, except during the rainy season; it is often connected to an **oasis**.)

For about six months, from March through August, a strong wind called a *shammal* blows in a northwesterly direction. The *shammal* can cause violent dust storms, which sweep across the Arabian Peninsula. These storms sometimes blot out the sun, causing wind damage and disrupting transportation and other services.

A TRULY DESERT LAND

Because the region is so dry and barren, Qatar has virtually no agricultural land of its own. Only 1 percent of the land area is considered arable, or suitable for farming. Although the government has tried to encourage agriculture and fishing, the people of Qatar remain very dependent on food ***imports***.

An even more serious problem in this desert land is the lack of water. Although some water is available in underground aquifers, this water is not ideal for either drinking or irrigation because it contains high levels of minerals. Another problem is that because of the need for fresh water, groundwater is being pumped out of the aquifers faster than it can be replenished naturally. According to a 1996 study by the Food and Agriculture Organization of the United Nations, Qatar's aquifers "will be depleted in 20 to 30 years at recent rates of groundwater withdrawal." And as water is taken from the aquifers the water that remains is often degraded. Salt water can seep into the aquifers, making the water brackish, and increased development in both the urban and rural areas of Qatar has caused some aquifers to become polluted.

The Geography of Qatar

Location: Middle East, peninsula bordering the Arabian Gulf and Saudi Arabia
Area: slightly smaller than Connecticut
   total: 4,416 square miles (11,437 sq km)
   land: 4,416 square miles (11,437 sq km)
   water: 0 sq miles
Borders: Saudi Arabia, 37 miles (60 km)
Climate: desert; hot, dry; humid in summer
Terrain: mostly flat and barren desert covered with loose sand and gravel
Elevation extremes:
   lowest point: Arabian Gulf—0 feet
   highest point: Qurayn Abu al Bawl—338 feet (103 meters)
Natural hazards: heat, dust storms and sandstorms

Source: Adapted from CIA World Factbook, 2002.

Water runs through the Wadi Bidiah, near Doha. Wadis are dry riverbeds that become filled with water after Qatar's occasional rainstorms.

The scarcity of *potable* water has restricted the extent to which the population of Qatar can grow, and the amount of agricultural and industrial development the country could support. To increase the amount of water available in the country, Qatar has begun desalinization projects, which manage the process of distilling seawater in order to remove its salt and make it into fresh water suitable for human consumption. Today most of Qatar's water is obtained through desalinization.

A problem with desalinization is the cost. It is expensive to produce the required amount of drinking water *and* enough fresh water to use in the country's agriculture (although the amount needed for farming is relatively insignificant because of the barrenness of Qatar). Additional costs are incurred to transport the water to all of the places where it is needed. However, the government of Qatar has been willing to pay these expenses so that its people can survive on this thumb-shaped patch of desert land. The emir has used oil revenues to pay for the desalinization plants, and the network needed to distribute water throughout the country.

In the spring of 2002, the government began construction of a $718-million facility that would take the salt out of sea water

A desalinization plant on the coast of the Arabian Gulf. Desalinization—the process of distilling seawater to make it fresh and drinkable—is expensive but necessary for survival in the country's desert climate. Revenue from Qatar's oil and natural gas provide enough money to make desalinization worthwhile.

> **Qatar and Bahrain were once joined, but the two land masses drifted apart over the centuries.**

while generating electrical power. The Ras Laffan power and water project is expected to eventually provide 1,500 megawatts of power and 40 million gallons of desalinated sea water each day. Several foreign companies—including the U.S.-based AES Corporation, which owns a 55 percent stake in the facility, and the Kuwait-based Gulf Investment Corporation—have invested in the facility. The Ras Laffan project was the first in which Qatar's government allowed foreign companies to invest in a local water projects.

PLANTS AND ANIMALS

Because of its desert climate, Qatar does not have much vegetation. Among the few plants that do grow in Qatar are hardy desert shrubs.

There are also few animals native to Qatar, mainly such creatures as bats and sand cats. The houbara bustard, also native to Qatar, is a bird of prey that has adapted very well to life in the desert. When it feeds, the houbara can extract enough water from its prey—generally beetles, grasshoppers, locusts, and lizards—to survive. (This ability is shared by certain desert hedgehogs and sand cats.) The houbara has a mottled coloring, which allows it to blend in with the desert environment when at rest or feeding, but the birds are quite noticeable in flight, as their black-and-white patterns stand out against the stark desert sky.

Camels are, of course, seen in Qatar, but there are not that many other animals. Falcons are sometimes used to hunt houbaras, but falconry is not as popular a pastime here as it is in other Arab nations like the UAE, Saudi Arabia, or Bahrain, and it is almost unheard of to spot a falcon in the wild. Gazelles can occasionally be seen, although the oryx, a deer-like animal with long, straight horns, has disappeared from the wild. The raising and racing of Arabian horses is not common in Qatar either, because of the country's poor climate and lack of vegetation. However, an annual horse race, the Qatar International Desert Marathon, brings and horseracing enthusiasts from all over the world.

The marine life is limited and consists primarily of sea turtles, most of which are probably on their way to the richer waters of Bahrain or the UAE.

Qatari Prime Minister Khalifa ibn Hamad al-Thani watches a parade during a visit to England, July 1971. At the time, Qatar was still a protectorate of Great Britain; however, within a year the country would be independent and Khalifa ibn Hamad would seize power in a bloodless coup.

History

*T*he history of Qatar is in some respects similar to the history of other parts of the Arabian Peninsula. For thousands of years the world's greatest powers have been willing to fight to control this desert land. However, in many ways Qatar has developed far differently than other areas of the peninsula. Where civilizations were permanently established in such places as Oman, Bahrain, and Saudi Arabia, many people believe the Qatar Peninsula may have been uninhabited for lengthy periods of time.

ANCIENT TIMES

Evidence of human habitation of Qatar dates back to the Stone Age. At the time, the climate of Qatar was much milder than it is today. During the 1960s and 1970s, **archaeologists** found rock carvings and collections of pottery on the peninsula, which have been dated to around

4000 B.C. Ancient burial sites have also been discovered at Umm al-Mohammad, on the western coast of Qatar.

Around 2350 B.C. the Qatar region fell under the control of one of the first great Mesopotamian empires, that of Sargon of Akkad. Sargon's empire included all of southern Mesopotamia (modern-day Iraq) and may have stretched from the Mediterranean Sea (around present-day Lebanon) to the Arabian Gulf. Sargon's descendants held his empire together until about 2200 B.C.

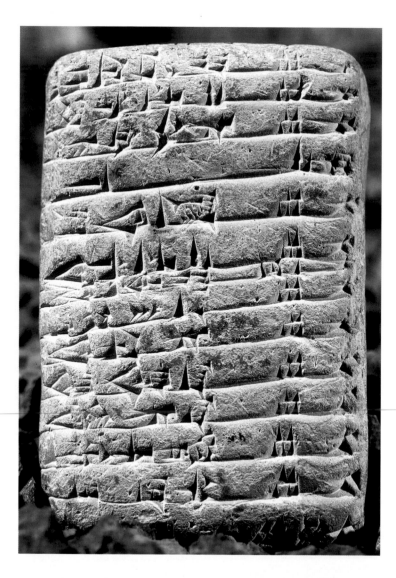

This clay tablet with cuneiform writing dates back to the second millennium B.C. (The writing on the tablet describes the monthly ration of grain needed for 17 gardeners.) For much of its history, the Qatar Peninsula has been subject to control by outside empires.

This carved head is believed to depict Sargon, the Sumerian king of the Akkadians, who ruled the Arabian Gulf region more than 4,000 years ago.

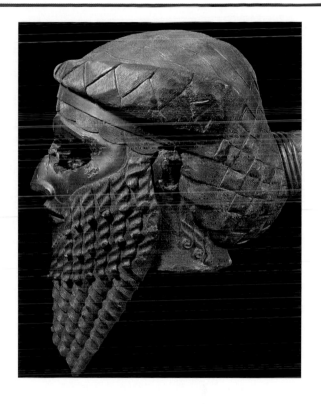

Eventually, the people living on Qatar became associated with the Dilmun civilization, which had emerged on nearby Bahrain. Dilmun was a city-state founded sometime after 3000 B.C. by exiles from an ancient civilization of the Indus Valley (present-day India and Pakistan). It held a key position on the trade routes between the Indus Valley and Mesopotamia. From 2100 to 1700 B.C., Dilmun was a major city, probably containing a population of between 2,000 to 4,000 people. Adventurers from Dilmun sailed their ships, called dhows, through the waters of the Arabian Gulf, the Red Sea, and the Indian Ocean. It was during this time that people living on Qatar began diving for pearls in the shallow waters of the Gulf.

Between about 1700 B.C. to A.D. 700, a number of foreign powers exerted control over the Gulf region. First, the Assyrian Empire, based in northern Mesopotamia, conquered a huge area stretching from the Mediterranean Sea to the Caspian Sea and from the Red Sea to the Persian Gulf. At its height, the Assyrian Empire was the largest in the ancient world at that time.

As Assyrian power declined, the strength of the Babylonians

rose. They took over Assyrian lands in the Gulf region around 600 B.C. However, they would not hold the territory for long. Within 50 years the Persians (from present-day Iran) conquered Babylon and made the Arabian Peninsula part of their powerful empire.

Around 325 B.C., the Macedonian conqueror Alexander the Great sent a Greek fleet into the Persian Gulf. Nearchus, an admiral in Alexander's navy, established a small colony on one of the Gulf islands (now part of Kuwait). After Alexander's death, the empire was divided among four of his generals; a general named Seleucus took control of the region that includes Qatar. During the rule of Seleucus and his descendants (known as the Seleucids), the people of the Gulf region prospered. However, by 250 B.C. the Parthians, another powerful empire from Persia, had forced the Greeks from the Gulf.

In the third century A.D., Persian control of the Arabian Gulf reached its highest point under the rule of the Sassanids, a Persian *dynasty*. The Sassanids ruled the area for about four centuries.

Qatar was just a marginal part of these ancient empires, and its people had little or no importance in their history. The only reason foreign powers were interested in Qatar was for its strategic location on the Arabian Gulf. They were willing to fight to keep their trade routes open. The peninsula was sparsely populated, although some fishing and pearl-trading centers developed during this time. The largest of these, Al Bida, was located near the site of present-day Doha.

RISE OF A NEW RELIGION

Until the 7th century A.D., the people of Qatar may have practiced any one of several religions. Some Arabs followed a variety of *polytheistic* religions, while others practiced Judaism or Christianity. The dominant religion of the Gulf, however, was Zoroastrianism (also called Parsee). This Persian religion had been

This fire altar was part of a Zoroastrian temple complex built in the second century A.D. Zoroastrianism was a popular religion in the Gulf region before the rise of Islam in the seventh century.

founded around 1000 B.C. by a man named Zoroaster (sometimes spelled Zarathustra). The religion's core belief is that the universe is involved in a struggle between the forces of good (Ormuzd) and evil (Ahriman). Ultimately, Ormuzd will prevail, in part with the help of man, whom he created to strengthen his forces. Zoroaster established three commandments—good thoughts, good words, good deeds—for the religion's followers to obey.

This began to change after the year A.D. 610, when an Arab man living in Mecca, a city in what is now Saudi Arabia, began to receive messages about the nature of God (Allah). The man was Muhammad and he was told to share the revelations about Allah with others. He began preaching to the people of Mecca, telling

This page from a 13th-century book in Arabic shows Muslims worshipping in a mosque. Most of the people of Qatar converted to Islam before the end of the seventh century.

them to give up their religions, particularly those involving the worship of multiple deities, and to obey the laws of Allah.

Ultimately, the leaders of Mecca did not appreciate Muhammad's message, and they plotted to kill him. When Muhammad learned of the plot, he and his followers left Mecca and fled to the present-day city of Medina, which was then a small village near an oasis. While in Medina, Muhammad continued to spread Allah's message and more people joined him. By 629, his flock was strong enough to return to Mecca and force it to surrender. Although Muhammad did not coerce the people of Mecca to convert to his new faith—Islam—many did so.

Muhammad died just three years later, after dictating the Qur'an (also spelled Koran), revealed to him by God. The new religion did not die with the prophet, however; it continued to spread throughout the Arabian Peninsula. In less than two decades after Muhammad's death, nearly all of the people living on the peninsula had converted to Islam.

As the people living in Qatar converted to Islam, they adopted a significant role in helping spread the religion beyond the Arabian Gulf. This was an indirect result of the peninsula's important location on the trade routes through the Gulf. At this time the people of Qatar were known for their skill at making both spears and cloth. They were also known for their weaving—particularly of beautiful striped cloaks—and for the quality of the horses and camels they bred.

The influence of Islam eventually spread beyond Arabia, moving throughout the Middle East, North Africa, and central Asia. During the next seven centuries, the caliphate, or position of Islamic leader, was held by two powerful families: the Umayyad, who ruled from 661 to 750, and the Abbasid, who ruled from 750 to 1258.

Qatar apparently thrived during the Abbasid period. Artifacts from the time of Abbasid rule have been discovered at Moab Fort in western Qatar. The fort itself is a good example of Abbasid architecture.

CONTROL BY OUTSIDERS

At the beginning of the 16th century, the region that includes Qatar fell under the influence of European invaders—the Portuguese, who establishing control over the Arabian Gulf and Indian Ocean. The Portuguese built forts and sent their warships to the region to protect their interests in the Gulf. This enabled them to control trade and navigation.

The remains of Portuguese forts can still be seen today in many

The arrival of the Portuguese in the early 16th century changed the balance of power in the Arabian Gulf region. Portuguese warships were armed with cannons, giving them an advantage over the Arab and Indian sailors they encountered. This enabled Portugal to build forts and maintain its presence in the Gulf for more than 100 years.

coastal areas of eastern Saudi Arabia, Yemen, Oman, the United Arab Emirates, and Bahrain. However, there are no significant Portuguese ruins in Qatar. That, plus the fact that the Qatar Peninsula was often omitted from maps made during this time and is not mentioned in accounts by travelers of the period, leads scholars to believe that the peninsula was either sparsely populated or uninhabited by the 16th century.

For much of the 16th and 17th centuries, the Portuguese were involved in a struggle for control of the Gulf with other powers, notably the Ottoman Empire, the Persians, and the British. By 1650, Portugal had been forced from its Gulf strongholds and the Ottomans and British each controlled parts of the peninsula.

The Ottoman Empire had risen in Turkey during the 14th century, when a military leader named Osman defeated other Turkish tribes to become ruler of a small kingdom. His descendants conquered the remains of the Eastern Roman Empire (or Byzantine Empire), taking the city of Constantinople in 1453. With this conquest, the Ottoman Empire became the strongest power in the Middle East. The empire would eventually grow to encompass the Muslim lands of North Africa and the Arabian Peninsula, and would expand into Greece, the Balkan Peninsula, and much of southeastern Europe.

Although the Ottomans claimed the entire Arabian Peninsula, their area of influence did not actually extend to the south of the peninsula. Great Britain, the leading European power during this time, had more influence in the areas of modern-day Qatar, the UAE, Oman, Yemen, and Iran. The British were interested in the Gulf because of their important colony in India. They needed bases for their powerful navy in order to keep the vital trade routes between India and England open. Britain also wanted to prevent its European rivals, such as France, from gaining territory in the Gulf region.

FOUNDATION OF THE MODERN STATE

During the early part of the 18th century, a tribe of nomadic Bedouins, the Bani Utub, left the central region of the Arabian Peninsula where they had lived and moved to the coast of the Persian Gulf. Their first settlement was in the region of modern-day Kuwait, where they found waters rich in both fish and pearl oysters.

The tribe was composed of three main families: the Al Sabah, Al Khalifa, and Al Jalahima. Members of the families divided authority over the settlement—the Al Khalifa would be responsible for the pearl trade, the Al Jalahima took control of fishing, and the Al Sabah became administrators of the settlement.

During the 1760s, the Al Khalifa and Al Jalahima decided to leave the village. They migrated from Kuwait to the northwestern coast of the Qatar Peninsula, where they established a town called Zubarah. The new settlement maintained a connection with Kuwait, and soon became an important center of trade and pearling. However, the Al Khalifa and Al Jalahima did not always agree on how best to run their settlement.

In the 1780s, Omani soldiers stationed in Bahrain attacked Zubarah. In response, the Bani Utub families of Qatar and Kuwait combined their forces and captured Bahrain. The Al Khalifa took control of the island, and eventually most of them left Qatar for Bahrain. There, the Al Khalifa established a dynasty that continues to rule Bahrain today.

This gave the Al Jalahima an opportunity to take control of the Qatar Peninsula. Under the leadership of Rahman ibn Jabir al-Jalahima, they moved to another location on the coast of Qatar and founded a new settlement, Al Khuwayr. They used this as a base to attack ships from Iran as well as from Bahrain, and Rahman ibn Jabir soon became one of the region's most feared pirates. However, the Al Sabah of Kuwait shifted their trade to Bahrain, and the

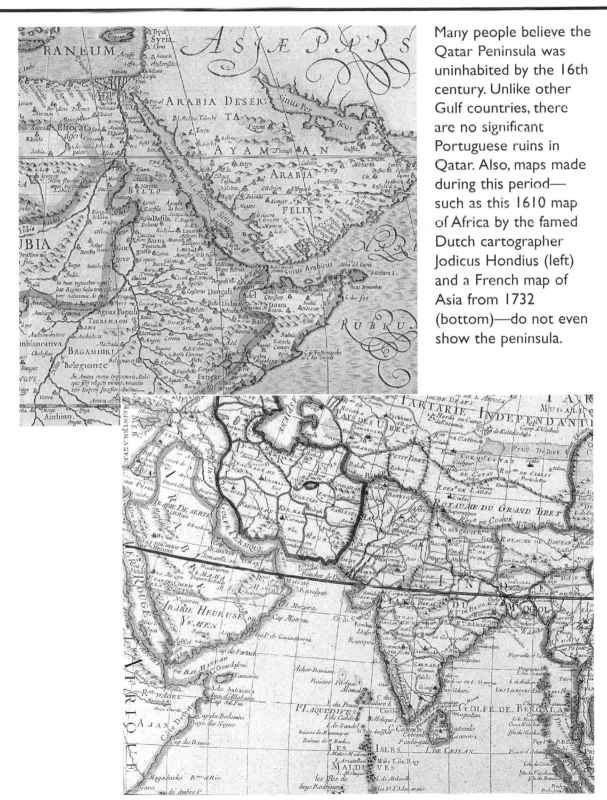

Many people believe the Qatar Peninsula was uninhabited by the 16th century. Unlike other Gulf countries, there are no significant Portuguese ruins in Qatar. Also, maps made during this period—such as this 1610 map of Africa by the famed Dutch cartographer Jodicus Hondius (left) and a French map of Asia from 1732 (bottom)—do not even show the peninsula.

importance of both Zubarah (which was still under the control of the Al Khalifa) and Al Khuwayr declined. Soon, the Qatar Peninsula was again unimportant and sparsely populated. The few remaining people built walls and fortifications around their villages to protect themselves from Bedouin raids.

By the early 19th century, the British wanted to end piracy and make the region safer for its ships. In 1820, Britain entered into a peace treaty with the sheikhs, or tribal leaders, living on the coast of the Arabian Peninsula. The British promised to protect the sheikhs from attack by the Ottomans or other powers; in exchange the tribal rulers were expected to crack down on pirates and give Britain a say in their relations with foreign powers.

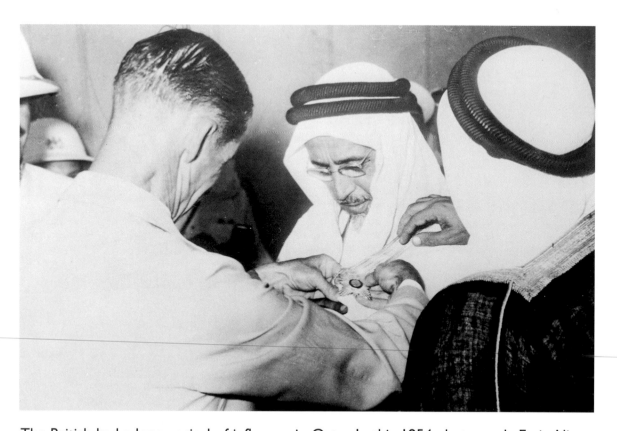

The British had a long period of influence in Qatar. In this 1954 photograph, Emir Ali ibn Abd Allah al-Thani (center) is made a Knight Commander of the British Empire during a ceremony aboard a British warship.

The British considered Qatar to be part of the Bahrain sheikhdom ruled by the Al Khalifa, and did not bother to make a separate treaty with the tribal leaders living on the peninsula. Therefore they were surprised when pirates based in Doha attacked British ships in 1821. The British sent warships to the region and bombarded Doha in punishment. However, sporadic combat would continue over the next five decades.

In 1867, an army from Bahrain sacked Doha and Al Wakrah. After a Qatari counterattack against Bahrain, the British decided to negotiate a settlement. Britain's political agent in the region, Colonel Lewis Pelly, arranged a peace treaty that for the first time recognized Qatar as a political entity separate from Bahrain. In the British view, the rightful leader of Qatar was Muhammad ibn Thani ibn Muhammad, a member of a strong Bedouin tribe living in Qatar. His descendants, the Al Thani, continue to rule Qatar today. The treaty between the British and Muhammad ibn Thani was signed in September 1868; this made Qatar a *protectorate* of the British Empire.

Muhammad ibn Thani opposed the Ottomans when they decided to reassert control in the eastern part of the Arabian Peninsula in 1871. After his death the next year, his son Qasim ibn Muhammad al-Thani submitted to Ottoman rule. However, Qasim was not satisfied with the Ottomans, and in 1893 he led a Qatari resistance that drove the Turks out of Qatar. Although the Ottomans continued to claim sovereignty over the area, they would never again have much influence in Qatar, and they ultimately renounced their claim to the peninsula in 1913.

When the Turks left, just before the start of World War I, the British recognized Abd Allah ibn Qasim al-Thani as emir, or ruler. A 1916 treaty between the Great Britain and Abd Allah ibn Qasim was similar to those entered into by the British with other Arabian Gulf nations, such the UAE and Bahrain. (The Arab sheikhdoms

Khalifa ibn Hamad al-Thani meets with Sir Alex Douglas-Home, the British foreign secretary, in London for a discussion about Qatar's independence, July 1971. Qatar declared its independence on September 3, 1971.

that signed treaties of protection with the British became known as the Trucial States.) In the treaty Qatar gave Britain control over its foreign policy in exchange for protection from attack and British support of the Al Thani rulers. A second treaty, signed in 1934, granted additional British protection.

INDEPENDENCE

For hundreds of years Great Britain was one of the world's greatest powers, with colonial outposts around the world. British power had been seriously weakened by the time the Second World War ended in 1945, however. The country lost India, an important part of its empire, in August 1947, and soon many other British colonies were clamoring for their own independence.

Although the leaders of the Trucial States were happy about the protection provided by their agreements with the British, Great Britain ultimately decided that with the independence of India, it had lost the main reason it had become involved in the Arabian Gulf region in the first place. In 1968, the British announced that they would withdraw from their treaty commitments in the Arabian Gulf region within three years.

Britain's initial plan was for the creation of a single Arab state from the Trucial States (Bahrain, Qatar, and the seven small kingdoms that make up the modern United Arab Emirates). This plan collapsed almost immediately because the individual states could not agree on how to share power in such an arrangement. Bahrain became the first of the Trucial States to declare its independence, in August 1971, and Qatar followed on September 3, 1971. The new country soon joined the United Nations, as well as the Arab League of Nations.

In 1972, the reigning emir of the State of Qatar, Ahmad ibn Ali al-Thani, was deposed by his cousin Khalifa ibn Hamad al-Thani. This ***coup*** had the support of other members of the Al Thani, as well as by the governments of Saudi Arabia and Great Britain. As emir, Khalifa ibn Hamad attempted to modernize the country by introducing new industries such as the manufacture of steel and production of fertilizers. But continued development of the petroleum industry would have the greatest effect on Qatar. Revenues

Qatar's current ruler is Emir Hamad ibn Khalifa al-Thani, who took power from his father in 1995.

from oil would change the tiny country from one of the world's poorest nations into a state with a modern *infrastructure*, services, and industries.

As in other Arab states where oil dominates the economy, Qatar's fortunes have followed those of the world oil market. In the 1970s, oil was a valuable commodity; during the 1973 Arab oil embargo, the price of a barrel of oil quadrupled from $3 to $12. This brought a great amount of money into Qatar's economy, leading to many development projects during the decade.

This prosperity was threatened in September 1980 with the outbreak of war between Iraq and Iran. Qatar and the other Arab states in the region initially tried not to take sides in the dispute between these two larger powers. In 1981 Qatar joined Bahrain, Kuwait, Oman, Saudi Arabia, and the United Arab Emirates to form the Gulf Cooperation Council (GCC). This was an arrangement for mutual defense of the Gulf states, but they also agreed to work together on economic development projects.

During the late 1980s and early 1990s, when world oil prices dropped, development projects in Qatar had to be canceled or delayed. Those years also marked a significant period of transition, as Qatar attempted to shift its economy from almost total reliance on oil. Today, oil revenues are supplemented by those from the sale of natural gas from Qatar's North Field, believed to be the world's largest field of natural gas.

On June 27, 1995, Emir Khalifa was ousted by his son, Hamad ibn Khalifa al-Thani, in a bloodless palace coup. Hamad was recognized as Qatar's leader by the other countries in the Arabian Gulf, as well as by several additional governments, soon after taking power. With his accession, Qatar entered a new era of modernization and reform.

Muslims bow reverently before the Ka'aba, a sacred shrine in Mecca. As in other Arab countries, Islam is the primary religion of Qatar. Most Qatari Muslims follow a strict form of the religion known as Wahhabi Islam.

The Economy, Politics, and Religion

Oil has impacted most aspects of Qatari life and has shaped its destiny as a nation. Qatar might have remained one of the poorest nations in the Arab world were it not for the discovery of oil in 1939. The money from sales of oil has provided a high standard of living for the people of Qatar. Oil money has been used to build roads, hospitals, desalinization plants, schools, and government buildings, and to make the lives of Qataris easier by providing free education and health care.

Qatar is different from other Gulf states because of its lack of successful merchant families, particularly before the discovery of oil. This is due to three factors. First, Doha's small size made it less significant than ports in Kuwait, Bahrain, or Dubai. Second, trade on the peninsula stagnated because of the absence of foreigners. People from India were forced out in the late 1800s, leaving Qatar the only Gulf emirate without Indians until the 1950s. Third, a single family, the Al Thani, has had a dominant role in the peninsula's political and economic growth. The Al Thani engaged in trade and in other enterprises. Sometimes, they used their family connections to win profitable contracts exclusively for themselves, or for firms in which they had business partnerships, such as with the Jaidah, Attiyah, and Mannai families.

A young girl stands at an open doorway beside an old merchant house. Qatar does not have the traditions of a merchant class as some other Gulf countries do.

The flag of Qatar is similar to the flag of its neighbor, Bahrain. Qatar's flag uses a distinctive maroon color, however, while Bahrain's flag is red; also, the white band at the hoist side has nine points on the flag of Qatar.

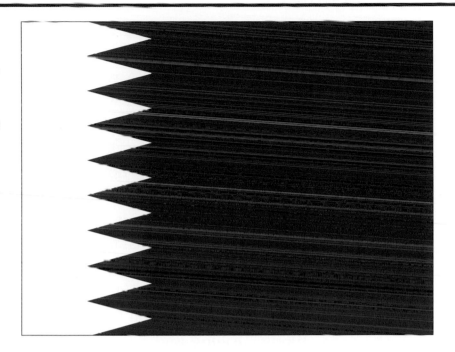

Although there were some Qatari merchants before oil, there was no merchant class to speak of compared to the ones in Dubai and Kuwait. Until the late 1930s, the two most important families after the Al Thani were the Darwish and the Al Mana. Both made their livings through trade, pearling, and smuggling, and competed for favor with the Al Thani emir. The Darwish and the Al Mana maintained their influence by giving money and advice to the emir in exchange for **monopolies** on trade and other concessions.

In 1935, a 75-year oil grant was given to Qatar Petroleum Company, a subsidiary of the Iraq Petroleum Company, which was owned by English, Dutch, French, and U.S. companies. Although high-quality oil was discovered within a few years, it was not until 1949 that Qatari oil was first exported. In 1952, the contract between Qatar Petroleum and the emir was amended, giving the Al Thani a larger share of the oil profits. During the 1950s and 1960s, gradually increasing oil reserves brought prosperity, large-scale immigration of foreign workers, substantial social progress, and the beginnings of Qatar's modern history.

During this time the Darwish family held a monopoly on the supply of labor, housing, water, and other goods to the oil company. This enabled the Darwish to reap huge profits. The Darwish monopoly ended, however, when workers, small merchants, and anti-British Qataris aimed a labor strike against Abd Allah Darwish, the patriarch of the family, in 1956. Because of the oil revenues, the Al Thani emir was not as reliant on money from the merchant families, so he did not need to break the strike to help the Darwish family. As a result, the once-powerful merchant families lost some of their political influence. However, the Darwish family remains very important in Qatar today.

Offshore oil exploration began during the 1950s and resulted in the discovery of several major oil fields near the island of Halul in the early 1960s. Drilling and production of offshore oil began in 1964. Today, oil revenues make up more than 30 percent of Qatar's annual gross domestic product (GDP), a measure of the total value of goods and services produced by the country each year. Of the approximately $11 billion exported from Qatar in 2001, oil accounted for 80 percent of the total.

Qatar's oil reserves are somewhat limited; in fact, some projections indicate they may be depleted by 2023. As a result, Qatar has tried to increase production of natural gas to help offset any future loss of oil revenue. In 1971, the North Gas Field, the world's largest field of natural gas, was discovered off the northeast coast of Qatar. The field contains more than 300 trillion cubic feet of gas, and is expected to have a productive life of more than 150 years. With this field Qatar has the third-largest proven reserves of natural gas—about 5 percent of the known worldwide total.

In 1974, the government began to **nationalize** oil and natural gas operations in the country. The Qatar General Petroleum Corporation was created to take over production and sale of oil and gas. (Today the company is called Qatar Petroleum.) By cutting out the foreign oil companies, which had taken a large share of the oil revenues, the ruling Al Thani soon became even more wealthy, and they used some of their money to make Qatar a modern nation with a well-developed infrastructure. Many people in Qatar have benefitted from the money generated by the sale of natural resources. The country's GDP per capita, a reflection of each person's share in Qatar's economy, is estimated at more than $21,000 per year, making Qataris among the wealthiest people in the world today.

MANUFACTURING: FERTILIZER, STEEL, AND CEMENT

Qatar's large supply of natural gas can be used to produce ammonia and urea, which are used in the production of

The Economy of Qatar

Gross domestic product (GDP*): $16.3 billion
GDP per capita: $21,200
Inflation: 2%
Natural resources: petroleum, natural gas, fish
Agriculture (1% of GDP): fruits, vegetables; poultry, dairy products, beef; fish (1996 est.)
Industry (49% of GDP): crude oil production and refining, fertilizers, petrochemicals, steel reinforcing bars, cement (1996 est.)
Services (50% of GDP): government, banking, tourism, education, other (1996 est.)
Foreign trade:
    Imports—$11 billion: petroleum products, fertilizers, steel
    Exports—$3.5 billion: machinery and transport equipment, food, chemicals
Currency exchange rate: 3.64 Qatari rials = $1 U.S. (fixed rate)

*GDP, or gross domestic product, is the total value of goods and services produced in a country annually.
All figures are 2001 estimates unless otherwise noted.
Sources: CIA World Factbook, 2002

commercial fertilizers. This has become an important segment of the country's economy. In 1969 the Qatar Fertilizer Company was established as a joint venture between the government of Qatar and several foreign companies. (Ownership is currently shared by Qatar Petroleum, which controls 75 percent of the company, and by a Norwegian company, Norsk Hydro.)

Qatar Fertilizer opened its first plant in 1973, with other facilities opening in 1979 and 1997. Today, Qatar Fertilizer is the largest fertilizer producer in the Middle East and one of the largest in the world.

Steel production is another key industry in Qatar. In 1974 the government of Qatar signed an agreement with two Japanese steel companies, Kobe Steel and Tokyo Boeki, to establish the Qatar Steel Company. The company soon built the first steel plant in the Gulf.

In 1997, the government of Qatar took over total ownership of Qatar Steel. The year 2002 marked the first time the company produced more than 1 million tons of steel in a year. In 2003, Qatar Steel began to expand its facilities in Mesaieed to ensure future growth of the steel industry.

Qatar Steel primarily manufactures low-carbon (mild) steel or medium-carbon steel. Low-carbon steel can be easily worked, and is used for many products from automobiles to pipes. Medium-carbon steel is strong and hard, but less easy to work or weld. It is often used for bolts, gears, shafts, axels, and pins. The most important of Qatar Steel's products is steel reinforcing bars. The company's steel products are sold locally and exported to other Arab countries in the Gulf region.

Another important product is cement, which is produced by the Qatar National Cement Company. The company was founded in 1965, and uses materials that are abundant in the desert—limestone, clay, and gypsum—to produce various types of cement. The main production plant is located in Umm Bab. Some of the cement is used in local construction projects, but most is exported to Qatar's neighbors.

AGRICULTURE

Most of the Qatar Peninsula is not suitable for agriculture—in fact just 2 percent of Qatar's land can be either cultivated or used as pastureland for livestock. As a result, farming is a small part of Qatar's economy, contributing just 1 percent to the country's annual GDP.

The Ministry of Municipal Affairs and Agriculture oversees farming operations. Qatari citizens who own arable land often work at

Arab dhows, or fishing boats, anchored off the coast of Qatar. Fishing has historically been an important part of the country's economy.

government jobs and hire immigrants to run their farms. Many of these immigrants come either from other Arab countries or from Iran and Pakistan.

Nearly all of the food produced in Qatar is consumed within the country. The most important crops are fruits and vegetables, poultry, dairy products, and beef. Because of the abundance of date palms, the annual date harvest is often very good.

Before the discovery of oil, some people of Qatar made a living diving for pearls. Although the pearl industry is practically non-existent today, fishing remains an important part of Qatar's economy. In 1966 the Qatar National Fishing Company was incorporated to oversee fishing and processing operations. Much of the fish—particularly shrimp—caught by Qatari boats is exported to other countries, primarily Japan.

POLITICS IN QATAR

The ruling family of Qatar, the Al Thani, was once part of the Tamim tribe that originally lived near an oasis on the eastern part of the Arabian Peninsula. The name "Al Thani" comes from the family's ancestor, Thani ibn Mohammed, the father of the first Al Thani sheikh to rule over the entire Qatar peninsula.

Democracy is the declared basis of the government, although democracy is not practiced in the way it is in the United States or in other Western countries. The state, as represented by the Al Thani emir, is responsible for maintaining the integrity, security, and stability of the country.

Qatar's 1972 constitution (sometimes called the basic law) declares that the country is an Arab, Islamic state with **sovereignty** held by the emir. Two other executive bodies help the emir to rule the country, the Council of Ministers and the Advisory Council (*Majlis al-Shura*).

The emir is the head of state, making all major executive

decisions and legislating by decree. The position is passed down within the Al Thani family. The current emir, Hamad ibn Khalifa al Thani, took power in 1995 with a bloodless coup that unseated his father, Khalifa ibn Hamad al-Thani. He has designated his third son, Qasim ibn Hamad ibn Khalifa al-Thani, as the crown prince, next in line for the throne.

Because the constitution gives the emir both legislative and executive powers, he has supremacy over the government. Among the emir's constitutional duties are convening the Council of Ministers, ratifying and implementing laws and decrees, commanding the armed forces, and appointing or dismissing senior civil servants and military officers. The constitution provides that the emir possess "any other powers with which he is vested under this provisional constitution or with which he may be vested under the law." This means that the emir can extend or modify his powers whenever he chooses.

The constitution also provides for a prime minister, who formulates government programs and exercises final supervisory control over the financial and administrative affairs of the government. The emir's brother, Abd Allah ibn Khalifa al-Thani, has served as prime minister since 1996.

The Council of Ministers is made up of the emir's top advisors, who oversee various areas of the government. There are 15 ministries in Qatar today: defense; interior; endowments and Islamic affairs; communications and transport; economy and trade; education and higher education; energy and industry; electricity and water; finance; foreign affairs; health; housing and civil services; justice; municipal affairs and agriculture; and official emir affairs. There are also eight ministers of state, who have specific responsibilities but are not in charge of a ministry. In addition to the executive role of running the ministries, the Council of Ministers also creates legislation, which must be approved by the emir.

Because of Qatar's natural resources and its strategic location, Emir Hamad has become an important world leader. Here he meets with U.S. President George W. Bush at the White House in October 2001.

The emir directs, supervises and coordinates the work of the Council of Ministers. The emir appoints and dismisses ministers, often with the advice of the prime minister. Only native-born Qataris can become ministers, and the constitution prohibits the prime minister and other ministers from engaging in business or commercial activities while holding office.

The constitution also provides for an appointed consultative assembly known as the Advisory Council. The Advisory Council can discuss the general policy of the state and express its opinions about new legislation or the operation of ministries to the emir.

Originally, the council consisted of 20 members, selected by the emir from representatives chosen by a limited number of Qatari voters. The size of the council was increased to 30 members in 1975 and to 35 members in November 1988. Among the council's constitutional prerogatives is the right to debate legislation drafted by the Council of Ministers before it is ratified and disseminated. Emir Hamad has promised to hold elections for a national assembly in the near future.

The members of the Advisory Council are selected from the country's nine districts, although the advisors are supposed to represent all Qataris, not just their home districts. The constitution originally called for regular elections for some members of the assembly, who would serve three-year terms. However, in May 1975 the elected members' terms were extended for an additional three-year term, and they have had their terms extended every four years since then.

In addition, the emir or his representatives hold regular meetings with the public (this is called a *majlis*). During the *majlis*, any citizen may address the emir or ask for a favor. For example, a Qatari may ask for a government scholarship so his child can go to school overseas. Someone else may ask for a grant of land. Sometimes, groups of people petition the emir to show their concern over a particular economic or social issue.

THE JUDICIAL SYSTEM

Historically, the emir's authority has included not only making the laws, but also **adjudicating** disputes and grievances brought before him. With the implementation of the constitution, a judicial framework was created in Qatar. **Secular** courts include a higher and lower criminal court, a civil court, an appeals court, and a labor court. All civil and criminal law falls within the jurisdiction of these secular courts.

Family and personal matters are the province of Qatar's *Sharia* courts. *Sharia*, or Islamic law, is based on the Hanbali legal school of Islam, in which judges (known as *qadis*) adhere to a strict interpretation of the Qur'an and other religious writings and traditions. At one time, *Sharia* courts had jurisdiction over all civil and criminal disputes in Qatar. However, since the 1960s decrees by the emirs gradually restricted the jurisdiction of *Sharia* courts.

As in the United States, the constitution of Qatar establishes the legal presumption of innocence (that is, that a person is innocent until proven guilty) and prohibits ex post facto laws. An example of the latter process is a situation in which a person were sentenced to life in prison for a crime, and the punishment for that crime were later changed to death. That person cannot be put to death for their crime just because the penalty was changed after their conviction. The constitution also stipulates that "judges shall be independent in the exercise of their powers, and no party whatsoever may interfere in the administration of justice."

Secular courts adjudicate based on the ruler's past decrees, and religious courts are restricted to questions of personal status. No provision exists for judicial review of the constitutionality of legislation, an important function of the Supreme Court in the United States.

RIGHTS OF THE PEOPLE

The constitution of Qatar includes a commitment to certain economic, social, and cultural principles that benefit the country's citizens. The state is responsible for providing health care, retirement benefits, and education to all Qataris. Programs for subsidized housing, pensions, education, and health care were started during the 1960s; these programs grew as oil revenues increased. Individual citizens do not pay taxes, and state subsidies keep the prices of food and other basic commodities low.

Programs like these stem from the emir's sense of duty, which is based on the obligations Islamic law and tradition places on Arab rulers.

The constitution of Qatar also provides a number of rights for the people of Qatar. These include equality among Qataris, regardless of race, sex, or religion; freedom of the press; sanctity of the home; and recognition of both private and collective ownership of property. These are similar to the guarantees set forth in the Bill of Rights, the first 10 amendments to the U.S. Constitution.

The year 1999 marked an important moment in Qatari politics, as Qatar became the first Gulf state since the 1970s to hold municipal elections. The nationwide election in March 1999 was for a 29-member Central Municipal Council, a consultative assembly that would work toward improving municipal services in the country. And for the first time Qatari women were permitted to vote, and to stand for election, in the municipal election. At the time, the emir commented:

> [This] is a big step towards enhancing the role of popular participation in practicing both executive and legislative action and establishing the basis of democratic practice in our country in a gradual way, until we ultimately reach the full democracy we dream of achieving.

The election was considered "free and fair" by international observers from the United States, Great Britain, France, and six other countries. Not everyone was as optimistic about the results as the emir, however. None of the six female candidates was elected, and one of them, Moza al-Malik, told the British Broadcasting Company (BBC) that she was bitterly disappointed. "It shows we remain in a male-dominated society to the bone," she said. "Husbands dictated who their wives should vote for. Women should stand by women."

RELIGION IN QATAR

Most people of Qatar follow Islam, a religion that emerged on the Arabian Peninsula during the 7th century. Islam shares several characteristics with two monotheistic religions that preceded it, Judaism and Christianity. The word "Islam" comes from the Arabic verb *aslama*, which means "to submit." The basis of the religion is submission to the will of Allah, as explained by the teachings of Muhammad. The Qur'an and other Islamic writings guide the behavior of Muslims in every aspect of their lives.

Islam is based on five basic precepts (sometimes called the pillars of Islam): *Shahada*, a profession of faith that there is no god but Allah, and that Muhammad was his messenger; *Salat*, a prayer Muslims perform five times a day, always facing the holy city of Mecca; *Zakat*, a charitable donation to people who are less fortunate; *Sawm*, the practice of fasting from dawn to dusk during the month of Ramadan (the ninth month of the *Hijrah*, or Islamic calendar, which is based on the lunar cycle); and *hajj*, a **pilgrimage** to Mecca that Muslims are encouraged to make during their lifetimes.

After Muhammad's death, a split occurred among his followers over who would succeed him as the caliph, or leader, of the Muslims. Muhammad's heir was his daughter, Fatimah, but according to Islamic law she was not eligible to succeed him because she was a woman. An assembly of Muhammad's advisors selected a man named Abu Bakr as the caliph. Although Abu Bakr was a close friend of Muhammad, and was the father of Muhammad's second wife, he was not related to the prophet by blood. This indicated that the Islamic leader would be selected by the strength of his faith, not because he was related to Muhammad. Most Muslims respected this decision. Those who obeyed the caliphs are called Sunni Muslims.

A smaller group of Muslims disagreed. They felt that the caliph should be chosen from Muhammad's descendants, and believed Fatimah's husband Ali, who was also Muhammad's cousin, should be the rightful caliph. They did not feel the Abu Bakr, or the two caliphs that followed him, were legitimate religious leaders. In 656 Ali was chosen by the Muslims as the fourth caliph. However, after he was murdered in 661, another caliph was selected instead of Ali's son. As a result, Ali's followers, calling themselves Shiites,

A view of the Abu Bakr Sunni mosque in Doha. The parking area is filled with cars because Friday is prayer day for Muslims. Most of the people of Qatar are Sunni Muslims, although in general they follow the religion less strictly than their neighbors in Saudi Arabia.

Rows of Muslims, wearing traditional dress, stand praying with their heads bowed outside the al-Hitmi Mosque, Doha.

broke away from the other Muslims.

Today there are more than 1 billion Muslims worldwide. Of that number, Sunni Muslims make up an impressive majority of more than 80 percent. Most of the people of Qatar are Sunni Muslims, and most Sunnis in Qatar follow a particularly strict sect known as **Wahhabism**. This brand of Islam emerged on the Arabian Peninsula in the early 18th century, when a religious thinker named Muhammad ibn Abd al-Wahhab said that Muslims had fallen away from the true faith. Abd al-Wahhab preached for a return to the fundamentals of Islam. He was particularly harsh in his criticisms of Shiites, who paid homage to shrines and saints. Abd al-Wahhab continued preaching against Shites until his death in 1765. His descendants and followers remained loyal to his quest. Among his followers were the Al Saud, the family that currently rules Saudi Arabia.

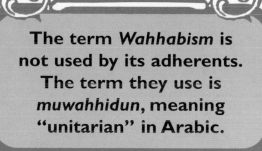

The term *Wahhabism* is not used by its adherents. The term they use is *muwahhidun*, meaning "unitarian" in Arabic.

The constitution of Qatar does not provide freedom of religion; Islam is the official religion of the state. Non-Muslims are not permitted to worship publicly, although Christians and Jews are allowed to hold religious services in their homes. The percentage of those who follow other faiths is less than 5 percent. Many non-Muslims are Hindus from India.

Two members of a Qatari soccer team try to take the ball from an Iranian player during their match in the Asian Club Championships. Soccer is one of the most popular sports in Qatar.

The People

T he people of Qatar are the descendants of Bedouin tribes that migrated onto the peninsula during the 18th century. In 1908, a British visitor to the area estimated the population of the Qatar Peninsula at about 27,000. Today, there are about 800,000 people living in Qatar. Only about one-fifth of the population actually holds citizenship, however. Most people living in Qatar are foreign workers who have been granted temporary residence in the country.

According to the U.S. Department of State, there are about the same number of non-Qatari Arabs living in the country as there are Qatari citizens. Non-citizen Arabs are primarily Egyptian, Jordanian, Palestinian, Lebanese, or Syrian, and make up about 20 percent of the country's population. Pakistanis and Indians each compose about 18 percent of the total population, while Iranians claim about 10 percent. Another large group of foreign workers, estimated at about 8 percent of the population, comes from the Philippines. There are some American citizens living in Qatar (about 6,000 in 2001) and there is a significant British community as well.

The official language of Qatar is Arabic, although due to the country's large foreign population many other languages are spoken. Because of the large number of Pakistanis, it is common to hear conversations in the Urdu language on the streets of Doha. English is also widely spoken in Qatar, and is taught during the last two years of secondary school.

Islam is the state religion, and the culture of Qatar is greatly influenced by religious practices. The workweek in Qatar is from Saturday to Wednesday; Qataris are not required to work on Thursday or Friday, the day of worship.

FAMILY LIFE

In Qatar, as in the rest of the Arab world, family ties remain an important part of the culture. Each family is part of a clan, or group of families, within a larger tribe, which can trace its history back to a common ancestor. In some cases, tribal histories may date back more than 1,500 years. Although tribes once differed from each other in language, clothing, and customs, these differences have mostly disappeared. However, Qataris cling to what

A folk dance called the *ayyalah* is often performed at traditional wedding ceremonies in Qatar. Accompanied by drums and tambourines, male dancers form two rows, which represent the clashing forces of a battle, and use camel sticks as sword props.

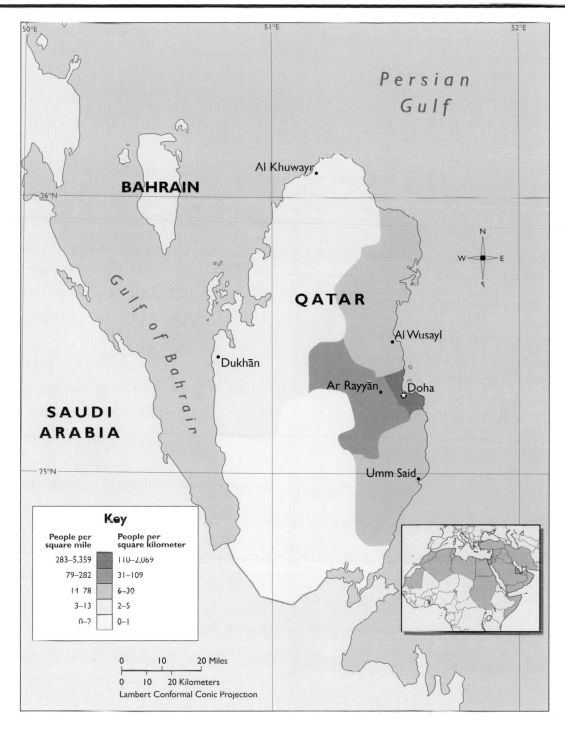

Most of Qatar's population is located on the eastern coast of the country. Doha, the capital, is the largest city; more than half of the country's population lives in or around Doha.

remains of their tribal identities, and people tend to marry within their tribe.

Often, marriage is not left to chance or love. Even today families arrange many of the marriages in Qatar. Girls are considered to be of marriageable age when they are about 15 years old, after they have completed their educations. Unlike in some countries, where it is customary for the bride's family to give a dowry to the groom, in Qatar it is traditional instead for the groom's family to pay a *mahr*, or "bride price," to the bride's family before the wedding.

Weddings are elaborate social affairs, and the celebrations can last for several days. Traditionally, men and women are segregated for their own ceremonies, which include feasting and dancing. The cost of a wedding can be tens of thousands of dollars. To reduce the economic impact, in recent years Qatar and other Gulf states have encouraged mass weddings, at which a large number of couples are married at the same time.

When men marry, they may leave their family's home and move into a house of their own;

The People of Qatar

Population: 793,341
Ethnic groups: Arab, 40%; Pakistani, 18%; Indian, 18%; Iranian, 10%; other, 14%
Religions: Islam 95%
Language: Arabic (official), English commonly used as a second language
Age structure:
　　0–14 years: 25.2%
　　15–64 years: 72.1%
　　65 years and over: 2.7%
Population growth rate: 3.02%
Birth rate: 15.78 births/1,000 population
Death rate: 4.34 deaths/1,000 population
Infant mortality rate: 20.73 deaths/1,000 live births (2002 est.)
Life expectancy at birth:
　　total population: 72.88 years
　　males: 70.4 years
　　females: 75.48 years
Total fertility rate: 3.1 children born/woman
Literacy: 81% (2000 est.)

All figures are 2002 estimates unless otherwise indicated.
Source: CIA World Factbook, 2002

however, in each family at least one man will remain at home even after he is married, in order to take care of his parents. When a woman is married she moves into her husband's home.

In Arab countries it was traditional that the husband was the head of the household, who made the important decisions and provided for the family while the wife was responsible for taking care of the home. This is changing in Qatar. It is not uncommon for both husband and wife to work, and for the household chores to be taken care of by servants. Many women in Qatar earn college degrees and go on to careers in business. Currently, there are more women enrolled at the University of Qatar then there are male students.

Although most Qataris follow the conservative Wahhabi brand of Islam, the Islamic laws are not observed as strictly as they are in some other countries, such as Saudi Arabia. Women in Qatar are permitted to drive—a privilege not enjoyed by Saudi women—and can operate their own businesses. Also, although Muslims are not supposed to drink alcohol, it is available in Qatar but not available in Saudi Arabia. And yet Qataris are strict in some observances. Most Qatari women, for example, dress themselves in accordance with Islamic law. They wear a *thoub*, a long black cloak that covers the entire body, and a *hejab*, a black head covering that shows only the eyes, nose, and mouth.

In public, men and women are usually segregated. There are separate facilities for men and women in mosques, government offices, and shops. Even at home, men and women receive guests in different areas of the house.

EDUCATION

Until the discovery of oil, there was no public education in Qatar. Most of the people living on the peninsula were unable to read or write; fewer than 10 percent of adults were literate in the

1940s and 1950s, according to a study done in 1970. Since the influx of oil revenues, the government of Qatar has done a lot to improve the educational opportunities for the people. As a result, the country's literacy rate has risen steadily, to 74 percent by 1985 and to 81 percent by 2000.

Today, education is free for all Qatari citizens. All children are required to have six years of elementary education (the equivalent of first through sixth grades in the United States). This may be followed by three years of preparatory education (middle school, or grades 7–9 in the U.S.) and three years of secondary education (high school, or grades 10–12 in the U.S.)

Secondary education in Qatar is intended to prepare students to either continue their studies at a college or university, to undertake technical or vocational training, or to join the workforce. Male secondary school students can choose to specialize in religious studies, commerce, or technical studies. Females are given initial training as teachers.

The government provides a free education for the children of Arabic-speaking foreign workers. However, many private elementary and secondary schools have been established for these students, or for those who speak English or other languages. Often, these schools follow the national curricula of a particular country— the United States, United Kingdom, France, Norway, Japan, the Philippines, India, Pakistan, Iran, Egypt, Lebanon, and Jordan, to name a few.

Students who wish to continue their studies beyond the secondary level have several choices. The largest university in the country is the University of Qatar, which is located to the north of Doha.

The university was an offshoot of a 1973 decree by the emir, which established a college of education to train teachers. By 1977, the University of Qatar was formed. It included the college of

A 1961 photograph shows children walking to school in Qatar. Before the discovery of oil, there were no public schools on the peninsula; children were educated in the home or at religious schools. With the growth of oil revenues, many schools have been built and education has become mandatory. Today, more than four-fifths of Qataris over age 15 can read and write.

education, as well as three other colleges, humanities and social sciences, science, and *Sharia* and Islamic studies. The university has since added three additional colleges: engineering, administrative sciences and economics, and technology. The campus is divided into two sections, one for men and the other for women.

Doha College, established in 1980, was intended to educate British citizens living in Qatar. The school's curriculum is based on the national curriculum of England and Wales. Currently, more than 700 students, representing over 50 nationalities, are enrolled at Doha College.

Qatar also has several schools just for women. The best known of these is the Shaqab Institute for Girls, which offers courses in art and general culture, family care and management, and physical fitness. The school is run by the Qatar Foundation for Education, Science, and Community Development, which was established in 1995 by the emir and his wife, Moza bint Naser ibn Abdullah al-Misnad. The Shaqab Institute is located in a historic fort, and is said to be the first institution of its kind in the Arab world.

The Qatar Foundation for Education, Science, and Community Development was also involved in the establishment of the Weill Cornell Medical College in Qatar. This was a joint project under-taken by the foundation with New York-based Cornell University. The program began in the fall of 2002, and the first doctors are expected to be graduated with Cornell degrees in 2008.

In addition, many Qataris attend colleges and universities outside of the country, particularly in the United States and Great Britain. The Ministry of Education and Culture provides scholarships to help students who want to study abroad.

SPORTS AND THE ARTS

In recent years, Qatar has attempted to develop itself as a destination for tourists looking for fun, excitement, or adventure. Today, there are many activities available in Qatar, from deep-sea fishing to sand-skiing on desert dunes. Sailing is a very popular pastime in Qatar, and each year the country hosts international regattas that draw participants and spectators from all over the world. Golf and volleyball are two other sports that are becoming more popular in Qatar.

One of the most popular sporting events in the country is the annual Qatar International Desert Marathon. The country also hosts an annual tennis tournament that draws major international players.

One popular sport among wealthy Qataris is the ancient practice of falconry. Training of falcons and other birds of prey is a Bedouin tradition that dates back to ancient times. Falcons can chase their prey for up to 3 miles (5 km); their modern-day trainers follow on horses or in off-road vehicles to be present when the bird snags its victim.

Perhaps the most popular sport in Qatar, however, is soccer. There are many soccer stadiums throughout the country, including 14 just in Doha. The national soccer team has earned a measure of respect in international competition; the team won the Gulf Cup in 1992, finished second to Saudi Arabia in the 2002 Gulf Cup, and

Tennis star Martina Hingis serves during a match at the 2001 Qatar Open. The annual international tournament draws some of the best players in the world.

reached the quarterfinals at the 1996 Olympic Games in Barcelona, Spain.

Qatar has an artistic tradition that dates back hundreds of years. There are many theatre groups in the country, including the National Theatre, which stages both ballets and dramas. The Doha Theatre Players Group performs English-language dramas.

At one time a *nahham* would be hired as a member of a pearl boat's crew. His job was to sing while others clapped and beat drums, in order to keep the crew members' spirits up during the dangerous trips. Many of the traditional songs are still performed today. In addition, folk singers and dancers still perform ancient dances at weddings and festivals. One of these is the *ayyalah*, in which the performers, holding swords, form two lines and pretend to fight a battle. Storytelling is another art form that has been preserved in Qatar, one that exposes Bedouin legends to contemporary generations. Some of the best musicians, storytellers, and dancers are members of the National Folklore Troupe, which performs throughout the country as well as at international festivals.

One of Qatar's most famous contemporary writers is the playwright Abdel Rahman al-Mannai. His best-known work is *Umm Zinn* ("The Most Beautiful"). He has also translated several English plays for Qatari audiences.

Qatar also has a long tradition of painted artworks, and the Qatari Fine Arts Society exhibits the works of Qatari painters. One prominent contemporary artist is Youssef Ahmed, whose work has been exhibited internationally.

Historically, Qatar has been known for its textile and weaving industries. According to ancient writings, the prophet Muhammad and his wife used fabrics from Qatar to make their clothes. Tents, rugs, cushions, and saddlebags woven in traditional Bedouin fashion from wool or from camel or goat hair can still be found throughout the country.

HOSPITALITY

In Qatar, as in other countries of the Arab world, hospitality is very important. It is a point of honor to make guests feel welcome. Guests are received in a special reception area of the home; men and women entertain their guests in different parts of the house. Traditionally, guests were seated on large cushions on the floors, although today it is more common for people to sit on sofas and chairs. Guests may be invited to enjoy a few puffs on the *gaudo*, a traditional smoking pipe.

Meals are traditionally served on a carpeted floor, and food is eaten with the right hand, even if a person is left-handed. (It is considered rude to offer something to another person with the left hand, or to accept something using that hand.) Meals usually begin with *mezze*, an appetizer; the traditional meal that follows often consists of meat (such as lamb or chicken) with rice or flat bread.

A young Bedouin boy stands near tents belonging to his family in the desert, Qatar.

A Qatar Airways jet prepares for takeoff. Since 1996, Qatar Airways has been the fastest-growing airline in the Middle East. The airline currently carries passengers to more than 40 airports, including such far-flung locations as London, Paris, and Hong Kong.

Often, food is flavored with one or more of the many strong spices available in the region.

Strong Arabic coffee, or *qawah*, is served both at the beginning and at the end of a meal. *Qawah* is unsweetened, but may be flavored with cardamom or cloves. The coffee is served in small cups that do not have handles. The cups are only filled halfway, and a polite guest never accepts fewer than two cups or more than three cups. Once the third cup is finished, it is considered appropriate for a guest to hold out the empty cup and tilt it from side to side, an indication that the cup should be taken away.

After the coffee has been finished at the end of a meal, it is time for guests to leave. Relaxed conversation is common before a meal, but guests do not continue to make small talk afterward.

TRANSPORTATION AND TECHNOLOGY

Qatar has a network of 764 miles (1,230 km) of roads throughout the country, 90 percent of which are paved. The country does not have a railroad network, but there are three important harbors—Doha, Halul Island, and Umm Said. There are also four airports, two with long paved runways for international flights.

Until 2002, Qatar was a co-owner of Gulf Air, a commercial airline that operates flights to other countries in the Middle East as well as to Europe, Asia, and North Africa. In that year, the country announced it would pull out of the Gulf Air partnership with Bahrain, Oman, and the United Arab Emirates. The government-owned Qatar Airways has grown rapidly since 1996.

Most of the people living in Qatar have access to telephone lines, radios, and televisions. Many people also either own personal computers, or have access to them through work or public facilities. Internet use in the country has risen greatly; in 2001 an estimated 75,000 people were logged on.

Doha is the capital of Qatar; it is also the country's main port and largest city.

Communities

Qatar is divided into nine administrative districts (*baladiyat*). These include Ad Dawhah, Al Ghuwayriyah, Al Jumayliyah, Al Khawr, Al Wakrah, Ar Rayyan, Jarayan al Batinah, Madinat ash Shamal, and Umm Salal.

The most important city in Qatar is Doha, the capital, which is located on the eastern coast of the peninsula. About half of the country's people live in or around Doha. Other large cities include Ar Rayyan (population 195,000), Al Wakrah (population 24,400), and Umm Salal Ali (population 19,200).

DOHA

When the Al Thani came to power in Qatar during the 1850s, they established their capital at Al Bida. This village grew into the city of Doha (also called Ad Dawhah), which today has a population of more than 318,500.

One of the most interesting buildings is the Government House, which was built in 1969. The emir's palace is also located in Doha, as are offices for all of the government ministries. The campus of the University of Qatar, and the headquarters for most of the major companies of Qatar, are also located in the capital city. There are three major roads that run through Doha, and most government buildings and office complexes are located near these roads.

An area of the city that is popular with visitors and natives is the corniche, a street that faces out toward the water of the Arabian Gulf. The corniche stretches for more than 4 miles (7 km), and is lined on one side with shops, restaurants, and hotels. Some visitors opt to take the 10-minute boat ride from the corniche out to Palm Tree Island, where there is a family entertainment complex, restaurant, and facilities for boating and other water sports.

A gas facility near Dukhan. This area on the west coast of the country is the center for oil production in Qatar.

Doha is home to a number of museums and cultural centers. The largest and most impressive of these is the Qatar National Museum. Its exhibits include displays on the peninsula's geological history, a fine collection of Islamic artifacts (particularly from the Abbasid period), and a maritime museum with examples of Qatari dhows. Other museums include Al Khor, a museum of anthropology; Al Wakra, a museum of marine life and natural history; the Weapons Museum, which showcases a collection of rare swords, daggers, and firearms; and the Ethnographic Museum, located in a restored traditional home, which shows how ordinary families lived in Qatar before the discovery of oil. A unique aspect of this building is its wind tower, or *badjeer*, which served to direct breezes into the interior of the house.

Two popular spots near the city are Doha Zoo and Aladdin's Kingdom, a theme park with rides and entertainment.

Other landmarks include al-Wajba Fort, located outside of Doha, which was built in 1882 and was the location of an important 1893 battle between the forces of Qatar and an Ottoman army. (The Qataris won.) Doha Fort was built in 1917, and today is a museum with displays of traditional crafts.

Doha is home to more than 250 mosques and places of worship. The largest and nicest of these is the Grand Mosque.

THE INLAND SEA AND OTHER INTERESTING AREAS

Khor al-Udeid (the Inland Sea) is an inlet where the Arabian Gulf twists into the peninsula in southeastern Qatar. Dramatic sand dunes, some as high as 131 feet (40 meters), ring the blue waters of the bay. Many people agree this is one of the most attractive areas of Qatar.

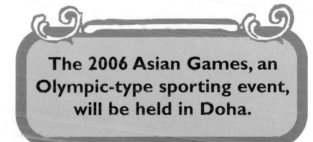

The 2006 Asian Games, an Olympic-type sporting event, will be held in Doha.

The Inland Sea is popular with undersea divers, bird watchers, nature photographers, and people who simply wish to enjoy its beauty. Campgrounds are located nearby, for those who want to spend time in the open desert. This is a popular pastime among Qataris, who go camping to get away from the stresses of city life and to remind themselves of their nomadic desert roots.

Khor al-Udeid is located 49 miles (78 km) southeast of Doha, but requires a four-wheel-drive vehicle to get there because the route crosses the open desert.

Just a few decades ago the Arabian oryx—a type of antelope with long horns and bold black-and-white markings on its face—was nearly extinct. In the 1970s, efforts to preserve the oryx began in several Gulf states.

The Arabian oryx was once nearly extinct, but the creatures are making a comeback thanks to preservation projects in several countries. In Qatar, herds of the graceful creatures are raised at the Al Shahaniya nature park.

In Qatar, a large herd is protected in a park near Al Shahaniya. Visitors who want to see these graceful creatures can either get a permit from Qatar's Ministry of Municipal Affairs and Agriculture, or take one of several commercial tours. While in the area, tourists often stop for the camel racing, which is held at a track nearby.

The al-Zubarah Fort, located 66 miles (105 km) northwest of Doha, guards an old port town. The fort was built during the early 20th century. It was renovated in 1987 and today is a museum. Five miles (8 km) to the northeast of the al-Zubarah Fort is another old fortification, the al-Shughb Fort.

Many other interesting forts are scattered throughout the country. One of the oldest of these is Murwab Fort, which dates back to the ninth century, during the period of Abbasid rule over Qatar. Archaeologists have discovered that Murwab Fort was built on the foundation of an even older fort. It is located just over 9 miles (15 km) north of Dukhan.

Burzan Tower is a unique-looking four-story watchtower that was built during the late 19th century. It is located at Umm Salal Muhammad, a small town about 15 miles (25 km) north of Doha. Another site of interest is a old mosque that has been restored, and the remains of some ancient mud-brick fortifications.

Umm Salal Ali, a town 25 miles (40 km) north of Doha, is famous for its grave mounds, which date back more than 4,000 years. People interested in Qatar's ancient history may also visit Al Jassasiya, on the northeastern coast, where prehistoric stone carvings can be found in the rocky hills nearby. Al Jassasiya and nearby Fuwairet are popular among beachgoers as well.

FESTIVALS AND CELEBRATIONS

The most popular holidays in Qatar are those related to Islam, particularly Eid al-Fitr and Eid al-Adha. Secular holidays include the anniversary of the emir's succession (June 27) and Qatar's independence day (September 3).

Ramadan, the ninth month of the Islamic lunar calendar, is the holy month of fasting. Adult Muslims are expected to abstain from eating, drinking, and other activites between sunup and sundown. After night falls, families gather to eat together.

Eid al-Fitr (the feast of fast-breaking) is a festival marking the end of Ramadan. It begins with the sighting of the new moon on the first day of Shawwal, the tenth month in the Islamic calendar, and generally lasts for three days. Muslims take part in communal prayers, either in a mosque or an open space outside the city, and everyone must offer charity to the poor. Friends, relatives, and neighbors meet in mosques and on streets, or visit one another, exchanging congratulations and small gifts.

Eid al-Adha (the Festival of the Sacrifice) takes place on the tenth day of the Islamic month, known as Dhul-Hijjah, The last month of the Islamic calendar. Eid al-Adha marks the end of the annual *hajj* period, during which millions of Muslims from around the world make their pilgrimage to Mecca.

The festival also commemorates an important moment in ancient history—the willingness of the patriarch Abraham to sacrifice his son Ishmael in response to a command from Allah. According to the Muslim account of the events, Allah was satisfied with Abraham's obedience to his command, and told Abraham to sacrifice a sheep instead. Traditionally, Muslims throughout the world slaughter a sheep in observance of this festival. One-third of the meat is to be distributed to the poor, one-third given to neighbors and relatives, and one-third eaten by the Muslim's immediate family.

In addition to these festivals, there are several one-day holidays that Qataris observe throughout the year. These include Muhammad's birthday and the date of his ascension into heaven. However, these are not marked by large-scale public celebrations as are the longer, more significant holidays.

Friday, known as *Yawm al-Jum'a* (the Day of Assembly) in Arabic, is the day of obligatory congregational prayer. As a result, Friday has a special religious and social significance for Muslims, and every adult Muslim man is required to observe the Friday prayer in congregation. For women, the congregational prayer is optional.

French president Jacques Chirac greets Emir Hamad ibn Khalifa outside the Elysee Palace in Paris before a meeting in October 2001. Since the 1991 Persian Gulf War, in which Qatar permitted the U.S., French, and Canadian militaries to use its air bases, relations with Qatar and Western countries have remained close.

Foreign Relations

As a small country surrounded by larger neighbors such as Iran, Iraq, and Saudi Arabia, Qatar might be expected to try to stay on the "good side" of its Gulf neighbors, just as Bahrain and Kuwait do. However, although Qatar has attempted to build and maintain strong relations with the other Gulf states, the country has not been afraid to stand up to its neighbors whenever it feels its interests are threatened.

The Iranian revolution of the late 1970s, and the Iran-Iraq War that began in September 1980, caused the Arab states of the Gulf to come together for security purposes. In 1981 Qatar, Bahrain, Kuwait, Oman, Saudi Arabia, and the United Arab Emirates formed the Gulf Cooperation Council (GCC), an organization dedicated to mutual defense and economic partnerships in the region.

Qatar's relationship with Saudi Arabia is complex. In 1982 the two countries signed a **bilateral** defense

Arab leaders participate in a meeting of the Gulf Cooperation Council. Six Gulf states formed the GCC in 1981.

agreement, and Saudi Arabia has been involved in mediating Qatari disputes with other countries, particularly Bahrain. On the other hand, since 1995 Emir Hamad ibn Khalifa al-Thani has tried to forge an identity for Qatar separate from Saudi Arabia. Though the people of both countries follow the Wahhabi form of Islam, its rules are considerably more relaxed in Qatar than in Saudi Arabia—a fact often criticized by Saudi fundamentalists. And the Qatar-based satellite television station Al-Jazeera has often found fault with the Saudi government, leading Saudi Arabia to withdraw its ambassador from Doha in September 2002 and to boycott a GCC summit held in Qatar later that year.

RESOLVING BORDER DISPUTES

In the early years of the 21st century, Qatar resolved a number of long-running border disputes. The most notable was resolution of Qatar's claim to own the Hawar archipelago, a group of 16 small islands immediately off the west coast of the Qatar peninsula. Although the islands are small, covering a total land area of less than 15 square miles (38 sq km), they are believed to be near rich undersea oil and natural gas reserves. The dispute between Bahrain and Qatar, based in part on the historical tensions between the ruling families of the two countries, was resolved in March 2001.

Both countries had claimed the islands during the 1930s, after oil was discovered in Bahrain, and began fighting over them in 1937. Because both Bahrain and Qatar were British protectorates at this time, the British government ultimately stepped in to resolve the dispute. In 1939 Britain declared the Hawar Islands to be the property of Bahrain.

During the 1960s, Qatar resumed its claim to the islands. The country's efforts to take control of the Hawar Islands intensified after both Qatar and Bahrain became independent of British rule in 1971. In 1978, the Qatari coast guard blocked fishing boats from Bahrain from entering the waters around the archipelago. Bahrain responded by sending its navy to enforce the rights of its fishermen.

The two countries nearly went to war in April 1986, when Qatari troops landed on the island of Fasht ad-Dibal and captured 29 Bahraini workers building a coast guard station there. Both Bahrain and Qatar mobilized their military forces, and an armed conflict seemed imminent. This was averted when diplomats from Saudi Arabia and Oman negotiated an end to the crisis. The captured workers were released within two weeks, and by June 1986 both Qatar and Bahrain had withdrawn their troops.

In 1991 Qatar submitted the case for its claim on the Hawar Islands to the International Court of Justice at The Hague, the Netherlands. Bahrain, which had hoped the issue could be resolved locally, also submitted a case to the court, which is the judicial arm of the United Nations. Bahrain also claimed a city on the Qatar Peninsula, Zubarah, which had belonged to Bahrain's ruling Al Khalifa family in the 18th century.

In March 2001, the International Court of Justice ruled that Bahrain would have sovereignty over the Hawar Islands. However, Zubarah, Fasht ad-Dibal, and Jinan Island were determined to belong to Qatar. In addition, the court declared that the waters between Bahrain and the Hawar Islands would be open to all ships. Control of Fasht ad-Dibal was particularly important to Qatar, because of its proximity to the North Field, the country's largest source for natural gas.

In the aftermath of the court's decision, the leaders of both countries spoke of building closer relations. Plans to build a ***cause-way*** that would link Bahrain and Qatar, much like one that connects Bahrain to Saudi Arabia, are being discussed.

Less than a week after the Hawar dispute was resolved, officials from Qatar and Saudi Arabia signed an agreement setting the border between the two countries. This agreement officially ended another long-running disagreement, which, like the Hawar Islands dispute, had once nearly led to war.

Qatar's border with Saudi Arabia had been established in 1965, when the country was still a British protectorate. After Qatar became independent the emir's new government never officially ratified the border agreement. The British-negotiated agreement already in place was observed without change for many years. The border area itself is mostly desert, through which Bedouin still roam, although there may be oil under the sands.

In September 1992 an attack on a Qatari border station left two people dead and a third captured. Qatar accused Saudi Arabia of the attack, and in protest voided the 1965 agreement. It also withdrew its troops from the Gulf Cooperation Council's defense force, which, though based in Kuwait at the time, was dominated by the Saudis.

Saudi Arabia claimed it was not responsible for the incident, and called it an isolated attack by Bedouins. However, mediators from Kuwait and Egypt were required to defuse the crisis between the two countries. In December 1992 Emir Khalifa and King Fahd of Saudi Arabia set up a committee to establish the border between the two countries.

Despite two border skirmishes during 1994, which led Qatar to

Saudi Arabia's de facto ruler, Crown Prince Abdullah, meets Qatari Emir Hamad ibn Khalifa in Doha. Saudi Arabia and Qatar have a close relationship, but one that has at times been strained.

boycott a GCC meeting in Saudi Arabia in protest, relations remained open between the two countries. In 1999 Qatar and Saudi Arabia agreed to divide the potentially oil-rich Dohat Salwa region, and signed maps that **demarcate** the boundary. Their foreign ministers signed the formal border agreement on March 21, 2001.

THE RISE OF AL-JAZEERA TELEVISION

Like most of the Arab states, the government of Qatar traditionally censored the media, quashing reports that were unflattering to the Al Thani regime or to the ruling groups of other Arab states. This changed after Hamad ibn Khalifa al-Thani took over control of Qatar in a bloodless coup in June 1995. Emir Hamad lifted some of the censorship restrictions on the Qatari media, and abolished the official Ministry of Information. Most importantly, his government granted $140 million over five years for the institution of independent satellite television news channel, Al-Jazeera (in Arabic, "the Peninsula").

Although each of the Arab countries has an official, government-run, television station, Al-Jazeera quickly became one of the most popular media outlets in the Arab world because of its news coverage and opinion programs, which go far beyond the boundaries previously permitted by Arab television. Al-Jazeera has never hesitated to criticize the governments of other Arab states, Israel, and the United States, and programs like *al-Ittijah al-Muaks* ("The Opposite Direction") have fostered debate on such topics as the failures of Arab regimes, the lack of freedom in the Arab world, and the need for changes to traditional Islamic law so that women have more rights.

Al-Jazeera's provocative reporting has led to a number of diplomatic crises between Qatar and other Arab countries. Saudi Arabia, Tunisia, and Libya briefly recalled their ambassadors from Doha because of programs they perceived as negative, and Kuwait and Jordan have closed Al-Jazeera news bureaus in their countries for the same reason. Israel has protested that the station has a pro-Palestinian slant because Al-Jazeera news reports referred to Palestinian suicide bombers as "martyrs," while Palestinian leaders have protested the station's airing of interviews with Israeli officials, such as Ehud Barak, Shimon Peres, and David Bar-Illan, an advisor to Israeli hard-liner Benjamin Netanyahu, the former prime minister.

Even Western nations have criticized Al-Jazeera. After the September 11, 2001, terrorist attacks on the World Trade Center building in New York City and the Pentagon in Washington, D.C., representatives of the United States criticized the station's broadcasts about the attacks and the subsequent U.S. effort to destroy the al-Qaeda terrorist network and overthrow the Taliban government in Afghanistan. U.S. Secretary of State Colin Powell attacked the station for airing "vitriolic, irresponsible kinds of statements," and newspapers in the United Kingdom called the station a "mouthpiece" for al-Qaeda leader Osama bin Laden.

Although many observers in the West feel that the station's coverage of stories in foreign countries is fair, Al-Jazeera has been criticized for not turning the same critical eye on policies and events inside Qatar. Al-Jazeera correspondents have reported when other Arab governments have made financial or political arrangements with Israel, for example, but were silent when Qatar opened a trade office in Tel Aviv. The station has also downplayed the fact that Qatar offered to let the United States military use its air base facilities to support an invasion of Iraq—a controversial decision in the Arab world. It particularly sparked controversy after Saudi Arabia resisted the U.S. request. As university professor Khalid al-Dakhil told National Public Radio in November 2002, "You will notice that Al-Jazeera always target[s] Egypt and Saudi Arabia, the largest states in the region, exposing their positions. These states, they have so many things to hide. The Qataris, they want to expose them, to distract

Qatari pilots fly their French-made Mirage jet fighters in formation with French, Canadian, and U.S. pilots during the 1991 Gulf War. Qatar joined a coalition of more than 30 other countries to force the Iraqi armies of Saddam Hussein to withdraw from Kuwait.

attention of the people from what they are doing themselves."

Despite the criticism it receives, Al-Jazeera remains an influential source of information and shaper of opinions in the Arab world. The station operates around the clock, broadcasting to more than 35 million viewers who are located throughout the Middle East, Europe, and even in some areas of the United States.

QATAR AND THE WEST

Qatar's relationship with the United States has gotten stronger over the past two decades. The U.S. established an embassy in the country in 1973, and a resident ambassador took up his post there in 1974. The State Department's Bureau of Near Eastern Affairs reported the following in Febuary 2002:

> Ties between the U.S. and Qatar are excellent and marked by frequent senior-level consultations in Doha and Washington. Qatar and the United States coordinate closely on regional diplomatic initiative, cooperate to increase security in the Gulf, and enjoy extensive economic links, especially in the hydrocarbons sector.

The warm relations between the U.S. and Qatar cooled in the late 1980s, when observers noticed U.S.-made Stinger missiles among the military equipment exhibited during a March 1988 parade in Doha. The U.S. government determined that Qatar had

Two high-ranking figures in Qatar's military, Lieutenant Colonel Hamad Ali al-Hinzab and Brigadier General Muhammed ibn Abdullah al-Attiyah, meet with General Norman Schwarzkopf and Mark G. Hambley, the U.S. ambassador to Qatar. In the aftermath of the Gulf War, Schwarzkopf visited Qatar and other countries of the international coalition that liberated Kuwait from Iraqi control.

illegally purchased the missiles through an unsanctioned third party, and demanded the surrender of the weapons. Qatar refused. The U.S. then suspended military cooperation and economic aid until the country destroyed the missiles in 1990.

Iraq's August 1990 invasion of Kuwait brought the two countries closer again. Qatar permitted U.S., French, and Canadian air forces to use air bases in the country during Desert Storm, the 1991 military operation that liberated Kuwait. Several thousand Qatari troops participated in the multinational coalition military force that

Emir Hamad listens as Israel Meir Lau, the chief rabbi of the state of Israel, speaks during a 2002 meeting of the World Economic Forum. At times during the 1990s and early 2000s Qatar seemed open to developing a closer relationship with Israel; however, protests from Saudi Arabia and other Arab nations prevented real progress from being made.

defeated the Iraqi army. The Gulf War marked the first combat experience for Qatar's army.

After the Gulf War ended, Qatar and the United States agreed to work together to protect their interests in the region. The two countries signed a bilateral defense agreement in June 1992, which gave the U.S. military access to air bases in Qatar and provided for U.S. and Qatari forces to work together in the event of a military conflict in the future.

Since 1992, other agreements have been signed that have expanded the U.S. presence in Qatar. Most recently, in December 2002, Qatar offered use of the al-Udeid air base, which has the longest runway in the Gulf region. The offer came after the Saudi Arabian government said it would not permit the U.S. to use its bases to launch an attack on Iraq.

By the end of 2002, the al-Udeid base was established as a potential command center for military operations in the Arabian Gulf region. In March 2003, U.S. warplanes used the base to fly missions against Iraq during Operation Iraqi Freedom.

Qatar continues to have a close relationship with the United Kingdom as well. Though Great Britain at times exploited the resources of Qatar—particularly oil—during its period of protectorship in the 20th century, its presence in the Gulf also resulted in profitable political, economic, and cultural ties. Today more than 2,500 British residents live and work in Qatar, and a number of British banks and other businesses have offices in Doha. Many Qatari students travel to the United Kingdom as well as the United States for college or graduate-level studies.

Among other European countries, Qatar has perhaps the strongest relationship with France. In 1994 the two countries signed a mutual-defense agreement, and a second pact was signed in 1998. In recent years French and Qatari forces have participated in joint training exercises aimed at fighting terrorism and at repelling foreign invasion. As part of the defense agreements, France supplies tanks, fighter jets, and other equipment for Qatar's military. According to some estimates, about four-fifths of the supplies for the Qatari armed forces come from France.

THE FOREIGN POPULATION OF QATAR

In many ways, Qatar is luckier than some of its neighbors in the Gulf. Countries like Bahrain and Kuwait have been torn by internal dissension over the years. Bahrain has a large population of Shiite Muslim ruled by a family that follows the Sunni branch of the faith. During the 1990s Shiites protested against the ruling Al Khalifa family of Bahrain, sometimes violently. In Kuwait, the government has alienated both the country's Shiite population and its more than 100,000 Bedouins, people who have lived in Kuwait for generations but are not considered citizens. By contrast, in Qatar Shiites make up less than 10 percent of the population. Also, they are free to practice their religion and travel to holy cities such as Qom, Iran.

However, Qatar does have a foreign population that is much larger than the total number of Qatari citizens, and historically the government has viewed this foreign population with some suspicion. During and immediately after the Gulf War, for example, thousands of Palestinian workers were expelled from Qatar because of Palestinian support for Iraq's invasion of Kuwait.

In recent years, the government of Qatar has promoted education, and has urged citizens who have left Qatar for an overseas education to return and take jobs in the country, thereby reducing the need for foreign workers.

CONCLUSION

Although Qatar is a small country, it is greatly important because of its oil and natural gas reserves, its strategic location in the Gulf region, and its willingness to work with the United States and other Western nations. Since coming to power in 1995, Sheikh Hamad ibn Khalifa al-Thani has made Qatar one of the most liberal Gulf states. Though it is still far from a open democracy, if Sheikh Hamad continues moving toward open elections, one day Qatar may be provide a successful example of democracy for the Arab world.

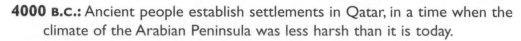

4000 B.C.: Ancient people establish settlements in Qatar, in a time when the climate of the Arabian Peninsula was less harsh than it is today.

2100 B.C.: The Dilmun civilization flourishes on nearby Bahrain.

325 B.C.: Alexander the Great sends a Greek fleet into the Persian Gulf, but dies before making significant conquests.

A.D. 228: The Sassanids gain control of Persia and soon spread their empire throughout the Gulf region.

610: Muhammad, an Arab trader living in Mecca, begins receiving messages from the angel Gabriel, and is told to teach the polytheistic people of the Arabian Peninsula that there is no god but Allah.

632: The prophet Muhammad dies, but Islam still flourishes, eventually spreading throughout the Arabian Peninsula and beyond.

900: During the Abbasid caliphate, Qatar becomes an important trading center.

16th century: The Qatar Peninsula remains uninhabited or sparsely populated for an undetermined time, according to scientists' findings.

1783: The Al Khalifa, who had migrated to northeast Qatar from west and north of the Arabian Peninsula, stop the Persian invasion and move their headquarters to Bahrain, while continuing to rule the area of Qatar.

1867–68: After the Bahrain-based Al Khalifa suppress a revolt by their Qatari subjects, destroying the town of Doha, Britain intervenes and installs Muhammad ibn Thani, from the leading family of Qatar, as the ruling sheikh (or emir). A British resident is given power to arbitrate disputes with Qatar's neighbors.

1872: Qatar submits to rule under the Ottoman Empire.

1893: An army under Qasim ibn Muhammad al-Thani defeats the Ottoman forces in a battle near al-Wajba Fort.

1913: The Ottoman Empire renounces its claim to the Qatar Peninsula.

1916: Qatar becomes a British protectorate after a treaty is signed with Sheikh Abd Allah ibn Qasim al-Thani.

1949: Oil production begins at Dukhan in western Qatar.

1960: Ahmad al-Thani becomes the new emir.

1968: Great Britain announces that it will withdraw from the Arabian Gulf by 1971.

CHRONOLOGY

1970: A constitution is adopted in Qatar, confirming the emirate as an absolute monarchy.

1971: Qatar becomes an independent country on September 3.

1972: Qatar's emir, Ahmad ibn Ali al-Thani, is deposed by his cousin, Khalifa ibn Hamad al-Thani.

1981: Qatar joins the Gulf Cooperation Council.

1988: Relations between the U.S. and Qatar cool after Stinger missiles, procured illegally, are seen at a military parade in Doha.

1991: Qatar forces join the United Nations coalition in the Gulf War against Iraq.

1992: Qatar signs bilateral defense treaty with the United States.

1995: Emir Khalifa is ousted from power by his son, Crown Prince Hamad ibn Khalifa al-Thani, on June 27 in a bloodless coup.

1996: The announcement of plans to introduce democracy in Qatar is followed by an attempt to assassinate Emir Hamad; Abd Allah ibn Khalifa al-Thani is appointed prime minister; the Al-Jazeera television network is established.

2001: The International Court of Justice rules on the long-standing territorial dispute with Bahrain over the Hawar Islands.

2002: Qatar signs a defense agreement with the United States, allowing an expanded U.S. military presence at the al-Udeid air base.

2003: Qatar holds its second round of municipal elections in March.

GLOSSARY

adjudicate—to settle judicially or to act as a judge.

anticline—an arch-shaped formation of stratified, sedimentary rock in which the layers bend downward in opposite directions from the crest. Its unique shape is caused by movements in the earth's crust.

aquifer—a layer of permeable rock, sand, or gravel that contains enough water to supply wells and springs.

archaeologist—someone who studies the material remains (for example, fossil relics, artifacts, and monuments) of past civilizations and cultures.

bilateral—used to describe an agreement that reciprocally affects two nations or parties.

causeway—a raised road that crosses water or marshland.

coup—the sudden overthrow of a government.

demarcate—to decide on a land boundary.

desalinization—the process of removing salt from sea water to produce drinking water.

dynasty—a succession of rulers who come from the same family.

import—something that is brought into one country or region from another one, usually for commercial or industrial reasons.

infrastructure—the system of public works, including power supplies, roads, and communications networks, of a country, state, or region.

monopoly—a situation in which one company or party controls a particular commodity or is the only provider of a service.

nationalize—to transfer ownership of a business from a private individual or corporation to the government.

oasis—a fertile or green area in a desert region where water is available.

peninsula—a narrow piece of land that juts into a large body of water.

pilgrimage—a journey to a holy place that is taken for religious purposes.

polytheism—the worship of or belief in multiple deities.

potable—suitable for drinking.

protectorate—a state or region that is defended and controlled by a more powerful state, or the relationship between the two states.

secular—worldly; not religious or spiritual in nature.

GLOSSARY

sovereignty—supreme power or authority, particularly over a state.

wadi—a riverbed that is dry most of the year, becoming filled with water only after heavy rainfalls.

Wahhabism—a conservative Islamic movement that is based on the teachings of the 18th-century cleric Muhammad ibn Abd al-Wahhab.

FURTHER READING

Cordesman, Anthony H. *Bahrain, Oman, Qatar, and the UAE: Challenges of Security.* Boulder, Colo.: Westview Press, 1997.

Crystal, Jill. *Oil and Politics in the Gulf.* Cambridge, England: Cambridge University Press, 1994.

Hourani, Albert. *A History of the Arab Peoples.* Cambridge, Mass.: Belknap Press of the University of Harvard Press, 1991.

Kechichian, Joseph A., ed., *Iran, Iraq, and the Arab Gulf States.* New York: Palgrave, 2001.

Lewis, Bernard. *The Middle East: A Brief History of the Last 2,000 Years.* New York: Scribner, 1995.

Ryan, Stephen. *The United Nations and International Politics.* New York: St. Martin's Press, 2000.

Shakir, M. H., trans. *The Qur'an.* Elmhurst, N.Y.: Tahrike Tarsile Quran, Inc., 1995.

Surrat, Robin, ed. *The Middle East*, 9th ed. Washington, D.C.: Congressional Quarterly Press, 2000.

Viorst, Milton. *Sandcastles: The Arabs in Search of the Modern World.* New York: Alfred Knopf, 1994.

Zahlan, Rosemarie Said. *The Making of the Modern Gulf States: Kuwait, Bahrain, Qatar, the United Arab Emirates, and Oman.* Reading, England: Garnet Publishing, 1999.

INTERNET RESOURCES

http://www.countryreports.org/qatar.htm

This web site provides tidbits of information and trivia about Qatar.

http://www.albawaba.com/countries/index.ie.php3?country=qatar&

A wealth of information on everything from Qatari history to geography. Also provides links to several news and media sites with Qatar-related information.

http://www.arab.net/qatar

This site presents brief paragraphs of information on Qatar—everything from its history to its economy. Links are also provided to other Arab nations.

http://www.qatar-info.com/consum.html

This is a great web site for anyone wishing to find general information about Qatar. It also provides information for those who are planning to travel to this country, offering practical tips on how to prepare and what to do when you arrive.

http://www.cia.gov/cia/publications/factbook/geos/qa.html

The CIA World Factbook provides statistical information about the geography, people, government, economy, communications, transportation, and military of Qatar.

Numbers in **bold italic** refer to captions.

INDEX

INDEX

PICTURE CREDITS

CONTRIBUTORS

The **FOREIGN POLICY RESEARCH INSTITUTE (FPRI)** served as editorial consultants for the MODERN MIDDLE EAST NATIONS series. FPRI is one of the nation's oldest "think tanks." The Institute's Middle East Program focuses on Gulf security, monitors the Arab-Israeli peace process, and sponsors an annual conference for teachers on the Middle East, plus periodic briefings on key developments in the region.

Among the FPRI's trustees is a former Secretary of State and a former Secretary of the Navy (and among the FPRI's former trustees and interns, two current Undersecretaries of Defense), not to mention two university presidents emeritus, a foundation president, and several active or retired corporate CEOs.

The scholars of FPRI include a former aide to three U.S. Secretaries of State, a Pulitzer Prize–winning historian, a former president of Swarthmore College and a Bancroft Prize–winning historian, and two former staff members of the National Security Council. And the FPRI counts among its extended network of scholars—especially its Inter-University Study Groups—representatives of diverse disciplines, including political science, history, economics, law, management, religion, sociology, and psychology.

DR. HARVEY SICHERMAN is president and director of the Foreign Policy Research Institute in Philadelphia, Pennsylvania. He has extensive experience in writing, research, and analysis of U.S. foreign and national security policy, both in government and out. He served as Special Assistant to Secretary of State Alexander M. Haig Jr. and as a member of the Policy Planning Staff of Secretary of State James A. Baker III. Dr. Sicherman was also a consultant to Secretary of the Navy John F. Lehman Jr. (1982–1987) and Secretary of State George Shultz (1988).

A graduate of the University of Scranton (B.S., History, 1966), Dr. Sicherman earned his Ph.D. at the University of Pennsylvania (Political Science, 1971), where he received a Salvatori Fellowship. He is author or editor of numerous books and articles, including *America the Vulnerable: Our Military Problems and How to Fix Them* (FPRI, 2002) and *Palestinian Autonomy, Self-Government and Peace* (Westview Press, 1993). He edits *Peacefacts*, an FPRI bulletin that monitors the Arab-Israeli peace process.

LISA McCOY is a freelance writer and editor living in Washington. She has had many articles published, and one of her short stories received an Honorable Mention award in L. Ron Hubbard's Writers of the Future contest. Her other works include *United Arab Emirates* and *Bahrain* in Mason Crest's MODERN MIDDLE EAST NATIONS series.